Dorian Williams is a solicitor of 30 years' experience who has practised exclusively for claimants in both personal injury and clinical negligence. He was instrumental in developing his law firm's reach in a variety of complex and challenging cases. More recently he has become a legal writer and educator involved in examining the advocacy of aspiring solicitors.

A Practical Guide to Claims Against Care Homes Related to Covid-19 in England

A Practical Guide to Claims Against Care Homes Related to Covid-19 in England

Dorian Williams, BA, LLM
Solicitor (Higher courts rights – civil)

Law Brief Publishing

Published 2025 by Law Brief Publishing, an imprint of Law Brief Publishing Ltd
30 The Parks
Minehead
Somerset
TA24 8BT

www.lawbriefpublishing.com

Paperback: 978-1-916698-81-9

PREFACE

It is now some 5 years from start of the Covid-19 pandemic hearkening back to very dark times for society. Yet it seems much more recent, perhaps because Covid has never gone away, perhaps because I have immersed myself in a retrospective. Whatever we may feel about this highly infectious virus, whether something to tolerate or forget, it has left its mark and will continue mutating.

Once there were the Dark Ages, much later the enlightenment, then the material age, now we are living in a pandemic age, or should that be now the endemic age? Definitions vary but the virus continues to cause death and worldwide numbers wax and wane according to the World Health Organization statistics.

This book arrives to set the scene on investigations into the handling of the pandemic by the government of the day. So it examines the ongoing Public Inquiry (UK Covid-19 Inquiry) and how that may assist those who wish to explore legal action. Baroness Hallett is chairing the Inquiry and is due to issue her final report by the summer of 2026. At the time of going to press, we have the first interim report of ten (reflecting the modules) on the UK's preparedness and resilience. All told, there are currently some 1,380 documents available to access (with much more to come); a documents' search on expert medical advice given to the government may be a helpful starting point.

There has been a Parliamentary Committee (Parliamentary Health & Social Care Committee) into the UK's Covid-19 Response. Their reported findings provide insight into the workings of government during the pandemic. They did not hold back, making trenchant criticisms of the delays in instituting lockdowns as '*one of the most important public health failures the United Kingdom has ever experienced*'.

One cannot disregard the significance of the *Gardner* case brought as a Judicial Review in June 2020 and heard in March 2022. The Claimants lost their fathers to Covid-19 whilst they were resident in care homes. The government via the Secretary of State for Health and Social Care was the Defendant, resulting in a partial but limited victory for the Claimants. The impact is still to be felt in how claims are pursued and won. Much was made of this reported case but will it assist as authority or evidence in the future?

Then we review the 'nuts and bolts' of framing a claim. Who will be the Defendant and what cause of action will be pursued? There are several avenues beyond negligence. Is their scope for breach of statutory duty in failing to provide personal protective equipment? It may be apposite to plead breach of human rights. What relevance does an inquest bring to an action? Expert evidence on medical causation will be revealed and may be persuasive. There is discussion about pre and post litigation procedure.

We may be on the cusp of substantial changes in the way cases are resolved and trials could become almost obsolete. Fixed costs apply to clinical negligence cases where full admissions are made in the Letter of Response. We can expect to see more admissions with significant time and costs savings. Behaviours are changing – or at least that is the hope – the Clinical Negligence Claims Agreement 2024 encourages a less adversarial and more cooperative approach. 2025 may well see fixed costs being rolled out for lower value contested claims; we have been here before – as applied to personal injury claims and anticipated shortly for clinical negligence. The figure of £25,000.00 has been mooted following governmental consultation in 2023. They were expected in April 2024 but with a new government, will their implementation be imminent?

And to the reader, I hope this book finds interest with practitioners, students and to those perhaps who have lost a loved one and are exploring whether they may have legal recourse. The book is skewed more towards clinical negligence but has relevance should a claim be pursued in personal injury. That could be an employer's liability claim for failing to provide a safe working environment, for example.

Finally, whilst the core of this book relates to the contraction of Covid or illness resultant from that, many people in care will continue to suffer from avoidable injuries that degrade their quality of life and dignity. Such could be physical abuse or failures to avoid pressure sores or fractures or inadequate nursing care leading to missed diagnoses. The pandemic naturally focussed resources on avoiding, diagnosing and treating Covid but others suffered too.

The law is stated to be accurate as at 1st January 2025.

Dorian Williams
January 2025

CONTENTS

TAKEAWAYS

- Limitation periods. Negligence: 3 years. Contract: 3 years for injury claim, 6 years for financial recovery only. HRA: 1 year. Judicial Review: 3 months.

  N.B exceptions.

- *Gardner* is unlikely to open floodgates of litigation. Judicial Review against the government was partially successful. The Policies of discharging patients from hospital to care homes was unlawful, allowing for asymptomatic spread of Covid. The HRA claim failed. There is no operational duty on government to take all reasonable steps to avoid an immediate risk to life arising from Covid in care homes.

- Negligence claims are the most likely cause of action. Asymptomatic patient admitted to care home and not segregated constituted a breach of duty (per *Gardner*). Actual or material causation of loss of life or injury must be established.

- No Inquest into a Covid-19 death unless culpable human failure. Where some failure of clinical care, thus 'unnatural', or cases of neglect or workplace infection/death due to lack of precautions, especially in healthcare area then Inquest required. Consider notification to Coroner. Evidence heard at inquest may assist in civil claim.

- HRA cases provide for wider range of Claimants – direct and indirect victims. Objective is to uphold minimum human rights standards. Not intended as compensatory, hence a different approach to an award of damages – 'just satisfaction' for violation of convention right is typically modest value. Causation has a different test than the common law. Defendant need only take reasonable measures to avoid risk. A high risk threshold to trigger Article breach. Claims against private care homes will have no standing (unless public funding by a Local Authority).

- Medical causation difficult in negligence suits (where/how was virus transmitted, multiple possible exposures?), less so in judicial review as Claimants need not show the guidance or regulations caused them harm.

- Claimant should examine precautions taken by a Care home to reduce transmission of Covid by application of WHO guidelines, early guidance issued by Chief Medical Officer and compliance with statutory obligations under the Coronavirus Act 2020, Health and Social Care Act 2008 (Regulated Activities) 2014 and Care Act 2014.

- Significance of 'six-pack' statutory duties in employers' liability claims against care home operators, especially PPE. Covid-19 deemed an industrial disease at inquest heard by South Wales Coroner in January 2023.

- Pre-action protocol for resolution of clinical disputes and CPR emphasise greater use of ADR and stocktakes to avoid litigation and promote settlement. More use of Part 36 offers. Front-loading of cases for early exchange of evidence and dialogue.

CHAPTER ONE

BACKGROUND

It is unlikely that anyone will forget the world's most recent significant infectious health crisis – Covid-19 that reportedly has caused over 7 million worldwide deaths[1] between January 2020 and December 2024, making it the fifth-deadliest pandemic epidemic in history. Another estimate says between 18.2 to 33.5 million excess deaths by April 2023[2]. There is bound to be under reporting. Whatever is the correct figure, by whichever matrix you choose – direct diagnosable deaths caused by Covid, or indirectly attributable to this disease, massive damage has been sustained to individuals, societies, economies and human development.

The top four pandemics preceding Covid-19 were the strain of influenza, known colloquially as 'Spanish flu', said to have killed between 17 million to 50 million people between 1919-1920; the first Bubonic plague ('Plague of Justinian') pandemic killed an estimated 15-100 million of the population in Europe between the sixth and eighth centuries; the second Bubonic plague ('the Black Death') killed 25-50 million Europeans between the fourteenth and early nineteenth centuries; and the HIV/AIDS virus has taken 43 million people over the last 43 years or so.

But the biggest killer over the course of time is likely to be malaria, possibly causing 50-60 billion deaths, or half of the human race. It continues to kill at least half a million people per year, despite the existence of effective life-saving treatment.

---

1 data.who.int

2 The Economist, www.economist.com/graphic-detail/coronavirus-excess-deaths-estimates

These bald statistics could well be under-reported as historical knowledge is sparse. Though figures for Covid-19 clearly will be more reliable but remain imprecise. Cause of death by Covid is difficult to assess, dependant on criteria applied. So official death records may include dying after a positive Covid test; those not tested may be excluded. Then again deaths of people dying from underlying conditions following a positive test may be included. People may survive the infection but suffer lost years of life.

Statistics of course go nowhere in addressing the incomprehensible level of suffering for those afflicted and their families – not to mention the risks borne by medics and frontline staff caring for those infected.

Approximately 227,000 people died in the UK from Covid-19 between March 2020 and May 2023, when the World Health Organization (WHO) said the '*global health emergency*' was over. Dr Mike Ryan from the WHO's emergencies programme said that '*In most cases, pandemics truly end when the next pandemic begins.*'

The point of addressing viral epidemics and pandemics is a reminder, if such be necessary, of the fragility of human life. And the need to ensure that wherever necessary we can ensure that health systems are able to respond effectively to crises and when (inevitable) mistakes are made that we all may learn from them –not least the government of the day – and try to ensure improvements are made. Such commentary is glib but many, if not all, will accept that serious errors were made in the handling of state measures in England to protect the public and specifically vulnerable and ill people in care homes.

I refer only to England because with devolved government, the other nations of the United Kingdom were responsible for administering their own public health services. This book will cover claims against care homes within England and Wales – Scotland and Northern Ireland having their own legal systems. That said, a measure of coordination was necessary between governments to mount an effective response to the public health emergency.

So *The Coronavirus Act 2020* passed with the consent of the devolved legislatures conferred new powers in health, education and justice to tackle the pandemic. The regulations were similar across the U.K initially, such as restrictions on movement and mandatory closure of premises and businesses. Importantly an indemnity for clinical negligence liabilities for NHS work in dealing with Covid was extended to those already not covered by the Secretary of State for Health and Social Care. However the act did not create new duties relevant to the management of health and safety.

In the interests of balance, because this book has no political remit, many would say there were some notable successes in the U.K, principally the rapid research and development, manufacturing and roll-out of a vaccine[3] that will have saved many, many lives (and continues to do so). But I will touch little on the successes because this book, as it must, will focus on omissions of care. It will therefore I hope be useful for those seeking guidance on bringing claims, rather than defending them.

Tragically, similar to cancer, almost everyone will have been affected to some degree by the ravages borne by Covid-19. Death, or on going disablement to 'brain fog', not to mention the impact on patients with other illnesses who may have lost priority to treatment are all consequences of the disease. And the economic damage and political recriminations – before one even turns to the prospect of litigation – add further to the misery. As will be covered later, the so-called anticipated floodgates have not yet opened, let alone been breached.

---

3 Oxford AstraZeneca vaccine research started January 2020; pre-clinical trials by Summer 2020 with roll-out to population in November 2020, following approval for use on 2.12.2020. Source: UK Research and Innovation.

1.1 COVID-19

In December 2019, there was a reported outbreak of pneumonia of unknown origin in Wuhan, China. It was observed that the Huanan Market in Wuhan was the main epicentre of a new virus related to the sale of wildlife at the market. It was concluded that there had been human-to-human transmission beyond the market. The World Health Organization (WHO) learned of the outbreak of pneumonia cases in early January 2020 and notified all country governments on 5th January 2020.

There is some scientific basis to suggest that this virus, later named as Covid-19 was derived from bats or some similar mammal. There is a majority consensus that this market was the likely origin, although there have been suggestions that the virus arose from a laboratory leak.

Whatever is the actual source, whilst hugely significant, does not feature furthermore in this book as going off topic.

We tend to think of Covid-19 as a known, specific disease, though it was only named as such by the WHO on 11th February 2020. The thinking being that CO represented corona, VI for virus, D for disease and 19 for when the outbreak was first identified (31st December 2019). The new virus was formally named as SARS-CoV-2. SARS being the acronym for severe acute respiratory syndrome. Covid-19 was declared by the WHO as a global pandemic on 11th March 2020 due to the rapid spread and severity of cases around the world.

Covid-19 is the respiratory disease caused by the SARS-CoV-2 virus, although interchangeably people do refer to it as the Covid virus.

A pandemic has traditionally been defined in epidemiological terms as *'an epidemic occurring over a very wide area, crossing international boundaries, and usually affecting a large number of people'*.

An epidemic is the rapid spread of disease to a large number of people in the population within a short period of time.

From December 2019, when cases were first identified in China, to the end of March 2020 when Covid-19 cases were found in nearly every country in the world, the evolving infectious disease became a pandemic.

The first case of Covid-19 documented in the UK was on 31 January 2020. This was a student in York that had travelled from Hubei, China on 6 January 2020. The second case was one of his parents. It is now suspected that other people had developed Covid returning from abroad as early as December 2019.

On 6 February 2020, there was a third confirmed case.

Coronaviruses are so named because of their crown-like shape of bulbous projections representing proteins emanating from the central core that look like a solar corona or halo[4]. Human coronaviruses were discovered in the 1960s, separately in the United Kingdom and the United States. They are part of influenza viruses. In fact they were cultivated using a common cold virus and given to volunteers which caused a cold and was inactivated by ether[5].

Coronaviruses have been known to cause infections in animals since the 1930s. The majority do so via the intestinal tract. All previous human coronaviruses have crossed over from animals.

Covid-19 is primarily transmitted between people by breathing or inhaling infectious particles. So that could arise through breathing,

---

4 See Tyrrell, Fielder (2002). Cold Wars: The Fight Against the Common Cold, OUP, p.96

5 Kendall, Bynoe, Tyrrell (July 1962), BMJ. 2 (5297)

speaking, coughing or sneezing. Transmission risk is highest within 2 metres of an infectious person.[6]

As will be evident, some coronaviruses are more serious than others; they can all cause respiratory problems, whether the common cold, pneumonia, bronchitis and some such as MERS-CoV can kill 30% of those infected.

There are six species of human coronaviruses, one of which is subdivided into two different strains. Four of them produce symptoms that are generally mild, while three produce potentially severe symptoms, namely:

1. Severe acute respiratory syndrome coronavirus (SARS-CoV), identified in 2003;

2. Middle East respiratory syndrome-related coronavirus (MERS-CoV), identified in 2012;

3. Severe acute respiratory syndrome coronavirus 2 (SARS-CoV-2), identified in 2019.

These coronaviruses cause diseases commonly called SARS, MERS and COVID-19, respectively.

If ever there needs to be a 'wake-up' call to the world about the proliferation of deadly biological disease, then it is starkly revealed by the fact that the three most serious coronaviruses known to man in the modern world have developed in just over the last two decades.

Of these three diseases, Covid-19 is exponentially far more serious to human life than SARS or MERS from the perspective that many, many more people have succumbed to the disease. The earlier diseases have reportedly killed low thousands of people compared to the figure of

6 See UK Health Security Agency on Covid-19:background information

over 7 million directly (or around 20 million indirectly) caused by Covid-19. The fatality rate for contracting MERS is 37%, 9.2% for SARS, yet a more modest 1.02% for Covid-19[7]. At its highest Covid-19 resulted in death of 1.35% of those it infected in the UK based on the infection fatality rate. For those aged over 75 it was reported as 12.8% and up to 19.3% for later variants[8].

That provides no comfort given the hugely disproportionate loss of life with Covid-19. One could surmise that it is much more transmissible between humans and therefore represents a far greater danger. For those first displaying symptoms and succumbing to death would take between 6 to 41 days, and typically 14 days.[9]

It is straightening to appreciate that given the comparisons with flu raised by some commentators and government officials, Covid has had an infection mortality rate 13 times higher than flu (in the United States).[10] However some caution needs to be exercised as firstly that was a US study and was in the early stages of the pandemic preceding any vaccine development. Nevertheless it underscores how deadly Covid was in the early months of this disease.

Health crises are increasing, not decreasing.

---

7 Covid-19 Dashboard by the Center for Systems Science and Engineering at John Hopkins University

8 Office for National Statistics, www.ons.gov.uk, Coronavirus (Covid-19) Infection Survey pilot:England, 14 May 2020; Birrell et al, www.mrc-bsu.cam.ac.uk/ 9.12.2021

9 Rothan, 'The Epidemiology and pathogenesis of coronavirus disease (Covid-19) outbreak', Journal of Autoimmunity

10 Pitlik (31 July 2020), Covid-19 compared to other Pandemic Diseases, Rambam Maimonides Medical Journal

Indeed Sir Jeremy Farrar, Director of the Wellcome Trust and currently Chief Scientist at the WHO, told the Public Inquiry into Covid-19 currently proceeding, that we are living in a pandemic age.

SARS-CoV-2 has a 70% genetic similarity to SARS-CoV. The virus has a 96% similarity to a bat coronavirus, so widely believed to originate from bats as well[11].

It must be emphasised that statistics for Covid-19 are gleaned in retrospect

The WHO announced that Covid-19 ceased to be an international public health emergency on 5 May 2023 after more than one year of downward trends in hospitalizations and deaths, accompanied by increasing immunity worldwide.

It is now probably considered an endemic disease rather than pandemic. So rather like seasonal flu where it remains ever present, somewhat predictable and static. Malaria remains endemic. The change of Covid's status is perhaps some cause for celebration (in that some level of control has been achieved in limiting its transmission through a vaccination programme), but recognising that it is likely to remain and cause death and suffering for a very long time. So yet another respiratory illness for the human race to contend with.

---

11 Cohen (26.1.2020), ScienceMag, American Association for the Advancement of Science

Chronology	(England)
8-30 December 2019	Patients in Wuhan, China develop pneumonia symptoms of unknown origin.
31 December 2019	Wuhan Public bulletin issued revealing multiple cases of pneumonia of unknown origin
5 January 2020	WHO notifies all countries and issues Disease Outbreak News notice
10 January 2020	China develops a laboratory PCR test to detect SARS-CoV-2 virus
11 January 2020	China releases genetic sequence of the virus
22 January 2020	Public Health England raised risk level from 'very low' to 'low' following reported case of Covid infection in US citizen returning home from Wuhan.
23 January 2020	Wuhan placed under lockdown and introduction of public health measures. Some countries instituted border controls to travellers from Wuhan.
23 January 2020	WHO reports evidence of 2019-nCoV (yet to be renamed) spreads from human-to-human
24 January 2020	WHO advises countries to institute exit and entry screening
24 January 2020	UK Government's 1st Cobra emergency committee meeting. Health Secretary advised risk to UK public was 'low'

30 January 2020	WHO declares virus a Public Health Emergency of International Concern. Risk level in UK raised from 'low' to 'moderate'.
5 March 2020	First death from Covid-19 in the UK
11 March 2020	WHO informs Covid-19 now a global pandemic – 118,000 cases in 114 countries
16 March 2020	UK Govt. guidance on social distancing and for vulnerable people
21 March 2020	WHO publishes guidance on Infection Prevention and Control for long-term care facilities
23 March 2020	National lockdown announced
26 March 2020	*Health Protection (Coronavirus, Restrictions) (England) Regulations 2020* enacted
10 May 2020	Lockdown lifted, though restrictions in place
28 May 2020	'Test and Trace' introduced
4 July 2020	First local lockdown in Leicestershire. Most hospitality businesses were permitted to reopen
3 August 2020	'Eat out to Help Out' scheme announced by Chancellor of the Exchequer
5 November 2020	Second national lockdown in England
2 December 2020	Lockdown ends after 4 weeks
8 December 2020	First vaccination (Pfizer) given to public

6 January 2021	Third national lockdown in England
15 February 2021	Hotel quarantine for travellers arriving in England from 33 high-risk countries
8 March 2021	Phased exit from lockdown
29 March 2021	'Stay at home' rule ended
17 May 2021	Most businesses (save highest risk) able to reopen
19 July 2021	Most legal limits on social contact removed

1.2 SPECIAL POSITION OF CARE HOMES

People staying in care homes typically will be elderly, perhaps frail and be clinically vulnerable and susceptible to infectious disease. According to the British Geriatrics Society (BGS)[12] the majority of residents are over the age of 80, most with multiple long-term health conditions with physical disability and cognitive impairments.

There were over 15,000 care homes in England regulated by the Care Quality Commission (CQC) at the start of the pandemic. Although they may not be described as 'care homes', there is also residential accommodation for younger people who are 'protected persons' who may not have capacity but are clearly vulnerable or those who have physical or learning disabilities who are in community care.

12 Prof. A. Gordon (and others), 'Covid-19: Managing the Covid-19 pandemic in care homes for older people', 18.11.2020

Residents of Care homes as defined by the CQC fall within four categories. Alongside each category is the approximate percentage of those users[13] residing in a Care home:

- Dementia (all ages) 45.9%
- Older person (aged 65 years and over) 14.3%
- Younger adults (aged 18 to 64 years) 13.1%
- Other 26.8%

It will be noted that almost half of residents suffered from dementia. This has implications about their capacity to give and follow instructions.

What was the scientific evidence base that was available to the government that may have informed its decisions aside from statistical modelling?

One was the Vivaldi project commissioned by the Department of Health and Social Care (DHSC) whereby a network of over 300 Care homes were studied early in the pandemic. They collected data on staff and residents of some 9,081 Care homes to understand the impact of Covid. It was estimated that there were some 293,301 residents with 441,498 staff. 56% of care home managers responded to the survey from which statisticians determined that there was at least one case of coronavirus in each care home that reported with an estimated 20% of residents testing positive and 7% of staff.

What they learnt revealed an increased risk of resident infection associated with the use of non-permanent staff, not paying sick pay for

13 CQC, Office for National Statistics

staff, new admissions to the care home, and difficulty in isolating residents.

Other research in observing Care homes involved the 'Easter 6' (later named the 'London Care Homes Network'). This involved genomic testing and contact tracing analysis to understand transmission networks in care homes.

Other than these studies, the government believes that remaining evidence on the impacts on care home residents has been indirect

According to the Department of Health & Social Care, initial priorities concentrated on trying to prevent ingress and minimise transmission. This resulted in trade-offs between maintaining staffing yet reducing transmission from staff moving between care homes. Stopping visits by family members reduced infection risks but also reduced the quality of life to residents.

Necessarily information learned as the pandemic evolved is retrospective with the benefit of hindsight. All will appreciate however that care home providers must institute all reasonably practicable measures to protect residents and staff. This book will explore to what extent that was done with the conflicting messages emanating from the then government in times of great upheaval and change.

There were especial challenges that the care home sector faced. Some of which included shortage of staff, lack of Covid testing and insufficient or inadequate PPE. Furthermore the design and layout of some care homes were such that segregation was difficult. Once an outbreak developed Covid could spread quickly.

On 3 March 2020, the government released its coronavirus action plan. This revealed its 4-stage strategy:

- Contain

- Delay
- Research
- Mitigate

SAGE (Scientific Advisory Group for Emergencies) had already advised on 10 February 2020 that it was likely that there was sustained transmission in the UK. Early on it was recognised that there were three main epidemics occurring – in the community; hospitals; and in care homes where transmission lagged around 2 weeks after high community transmission. An independent report published into the epidemiology of the pandemic in Care homes[14] commissioned by the government found that the majority of outbreaks of Covid were introduced unintentionally by staff living in the community. At this stage, Care homes were largely closed to visitors. Now this report is after the event and will not necessarily assist in formulating a claim unless such risk was foreseeable. It is stated that by the end of waves 1 and 2 at least a quarter of staff and a third of surviving residents had already been infected.

Deaths in Care homes peaked during the first wave in late March 2020. Registered deaths for the week ending 27 March 2020 were some 7750 with some 2500 having Covid-19 on the death certificate.[15]

According to the Office for National Statistics the first wave had the highest proportion of deaths involving Covid with a total of 19,783 representing 23.2% of deaths in Care homes. In the second wave 20.9% involved Covid amounting to 20,766 deaths.

---

14 www.gov.uk/government/publications/technical-report-on-the-covid-pandemic-in-the-uk/chapter-82-care-homes

15 Office for Health Improvement and Disparities: Excess Deaths In England

Within short order, some Care Homes decided to close their doors to visitors, with Barchester and HC-One stopping non-essential visits on 10 March and 12 March respectively. This was followed up by BUPA and Four Seasons care homes doing the same on 13 March.

The BGS first issued guidance on Covid in care homes in March 2020. Taken together with publications by the DHSC in conjunction with the CQC and the UK Health Security Agency on infection prevention and control, and on admission and care requirements (during Covid) will assist in determining duty of care measures and possible breaches.

The WHO issued its interim guidance on 21 March 2020 for infection prevention and control that covered care and nursing homes[16]. However it did not mention social care institutions that could house younger vulnerable individuals. The WHO recognised that people living in long-term care facilities were at a higher risk for an adverse outcome because of their age and physical and mental vulnerabilities due to living in close proximity to others. The aim of that document was to provide guidance to prevent Covid from entering the facility; to prevent the virus from spreading within the facility; and to prevent it spreading outside. This is a helpful document in reviewing allegations that may be put in formulating breach of duty or in support of a possible Article 2 breach. They advised as a minimum:

- Provide Covid-19 training to all employees, including hand hygiene and respiratory etiquette; standard and Covid transmission-based precautions.

- Provide information sessions for residents on Covid-19 to inform them about the virus, respiratory disease and how to protect themselves from infection.

16 iris.who.int

- Regularly audit infection, prevention and control practices (e.g. hand hygiene compliance).
- Increase emphasis on hand hygiene and respiratory etiquette.
- Maintain high standards of hygiene and sanitation practice.
- Ensure physical distancing, achievable by restricting numbers of visitors, staggering meal times, minimum 1m distance between residents/staff.
- Restrict access to visitors with screening for signs and symptoms of acute respiratory infection. Those who are admitted should be on compassionate grounds only.
- Surveillance of residents for Covid-19. Assess health status of any new residents at admission to determine signs of fever, cough or shortness of breath. Assess each resident twice daily for the development of a fever (from 38C).
- Surveillance of employees for Covid-19. Employees to remain at home with any fever or respiratory illness. Undertake temperature check of all employees at facility entrance. Monitor employees and their contact with residents.
- Surveillance for visitors should be established, namely screening before admission to see residents, including for fever, respiratory illness and whether come into contact with someone infected with Covid-19. Visitors with fever or respiratory illness should be denied access. And those visitors with significant risk factors for Covid, such as recent travel to an area with community transmission should be denied access.

The guidance sets out measures to be taken if a resident is suspected to have, or is diagnosed with Covid. That includes wearing of medical masks for both the resident and others in the room. The resident should be isolated and really should be cared for in a health facility – that really would mean transfer to hospital or to a nursing home with specialist facilities.

Contact precautions apply to those caring for a resident with Covid or suspected Covid so this requires the use of PPE – medical mask, gloves, gown and eye protection. There should be twice daily cleaning with hospital-grade disinfecting agents for all frequently touched areas.

Those with Covid or are suspected to have it should be confined to their rooms while ill. Isolation is advised until there are two negative laboratory tests for Covid taken at least 24 hours apart after resolution of symptoms. If testing is not possible, the WHO recommends residents remain isolated for an additional two weeks after symptoms resolve.

This could represent a fertile area for pre-action disclosure to ascertain the risk assessments and procedures that care homes should have had in place in the early stages of the first pandemic wave.

But the big question is whether the Government interposed the WHO guidance into its own recommendations. And if not, does that make them potentially liable. The starting point, it is suggested, is review of the government's initial guidance documents:

'Coronavirus (COVID-19): admission and care of people in care homes' first published on 2 April 2020[17]

'Covid-19 Hospital Discharge Service Requirements' published 19 March 2020[18]

17 www.gov.uk/government/publications/coronavirus-covid19-admission-and-care-of-people-in-care-homes

'Covid-19: Our Action Plan for Adult Social Care' published 15 April 2020[19]

'Covid-19: infection prevention and control (IPC) guidance published 24 April 2020[20]

The first document on admission to care homes expected that people discharged from hospital would be admitted, although the hospital discharge document had the proviso that they must be clinically safe to discharge. However that did not require hospitals to do testing. This policy was operational from 19 March 2020. The UK guidance does not recommend that a resident should be isolated until they have had two negative laboratory tests for Covid-19 at least 24 hours apart.

The WHO guidance is more rigorous than the UK guidelines. For example on PPE, residents should wear a medical mask in suspected or confirmed cases but the government stipulated that this was only required when residents were transferred between rooms. Eye protection was not necessary for cleaners or care staff, yet the WHO stated it was to be worn by staff within 2 metres of residents. There were no distancing requirements other than reference by the government to follow 'social distancing measures'; but the WHO required 1 metre between residents. The WHO recommended that meals should have been staggered to ensure that physical distance was maintained.

The BGS issued a good practice guide on 30 March 2020. This also differed from that issued by the government. PPE naturally featured; staff must wear recommended PPE for contact with all care home residents. This applied also to visitors, including family members. In

---

18 www.gov.uk (withdrawn document but still accessible though publications)

19 ibid

20 ibid

relation to infection control, national guidance should be followed or if not available then the 'Bushproof guidance' provides a summary of (then current) expert advice. The BGS recognised that Covid-19 is often symptomatic such that regular testing of care home staff was essential. Staff who declined testing should not have been involved in direct care of residents. They advised that care homes should not have accepted admissions from hospital until informed of a resident's Covid status. Where a patient had tested positive (under England's policy), a care home might have been asked to accept a Covid positive patient but only, according to the BGC where that home was approved by the CQC as a 'designated setting'. Even then, this will be subject to risk assessments based on resident care needs and organisational capacity. Significantly they suggested that all admissions to care homes should be quarantined for 14 days after admission.

Not all new entrants into care homes were tested in April 2020 despite advice from Sir Chris Whitty that this should happen. On 15 April 2020, the social care action plan was launched in the face of 400 care home deaths per day. Testing of staff and new entrants was to be commenced. This was revised on 28 April 2020 to all care staff and residents, regardless of whether they had symptoms.

According to the International Long-term care policy network (LTC)[21], they were critical of guidance issued particularly by Public Health England. They considered that asymptomatic/pre-symptomatic transmission was a major contributor to the spread of Covid-19, introduced from outside either from staff or patients from hospitals. There needed to be a clear demarcation within a care home of zones of risk, i.e. contaminated areas, possible contamination and clean (green) zones. Hand disinfection was necessary for all points between risk zones.

---

21 'Mapping of UK Government Guidance for Infection Prevention and Control (IPC) for Covid-19 in Care Homes, 15 May 2020, itccovid.org

Government guidance to care homes was not always clear, lacked overall coherence and failed to communicate sufficiently about the routes for transmission and how to block them. The document by Public Health England, *'Covid-19 How to work safely in care homes'*, dated 17 April 2020 gave helpful and simple advice on PPE, but was poor on other aspects of Infection prevention and control. It made factually incorrect statements on routes of transmission, likening transmission characteristics of Covid-19 to the 2003 SARS-CoV outbreak. It also stated that the incubation period was 1 to 14 days with a median of 5 days and similar to SARS, most patients will not be infectious until the onset of symptoms. By this stage, the international experience had identified asymptomatic transmission.

According to LTC, the biggest gaps within the UK government/PHE and the NHS were:

1. Failing to recognise the critical role that asymptomatic and pre-symptomatic transmission had in the spread of Covid-19 in care homes;

2. Lack of a coherent zoning approach to infection, prevention and control;

3. Insufficient understanding of transmission routes and not emphasising gloves on hand hygiene and also when gloves are off;

4. Focussing on symptoms of new cough and high temperature (which are not the most common for older people) in suspecting Covid; and

5. No one-stop document with clear, practical guidance for care homes to implement.

It has been thought that during the first wave, when the government encouraged discharge of patients into Care homes, that this was one of the principal causes of a spike in Covid transmissions. However some statistical modelling research[22] has indicated that a discharge from hospital into a care home was not associated with a significant increase in risk of a Covid outbreak. This was a study in Wales so is not necessarily applicable to the English experience. They found that the number of cases associated with care homes stopped rising following the requirement to test on discharge. They concluded that this suggested that alternative sources for seeding residential care outbreaks should be investigated. Some studies in England indicate that PPE and number of staff employed have an impact on the number of Covid-19 infections.[23]

1.3 STATUS OF LITIGATION

It had been thought that with unprecedented numbers of people dying or seriously affected by contraction of the Covid-19 coronavirus that litigation would be rife against the NHS and care homes, especially following the decision in *Gardner.*[24]

Claimants would be expected to be from those who had suffered infection and illness from Covid-19 and from relatives acting on behalf of the estate of a loved family member. Or it could be from those whose

---

22 'Risk factors for outbreaks of COVID-19 in care homes following hospital discharge: A national cohort analysis', 6 Feb 2021, Emmerson at al, pmc.ncbi.nih.gov/articles/PMC8013658/

23 'Introduction to and spread of Covid-19 in care homes in Norfolk, UK', Medrvx, 2020, Brainard et al

'Evolution and effects of COVID-19 outbreaks in care homes: a population analysis in 189 care homes in one geographical region of the UK', Lancet Healthy Longev, 2020, Burton et al.

24 (1) Gardner (2) Harris v (1) Secretary of State for Health and Social Care (2) NHS Commissioning Board (3) Public Health England [2022] EWHC 967 (Admin)

medical condition has not been diagnosed on a timely basis and a delay in treatment as those suffering from Covid were prioritised. Many would say that the NHS has been under-resourced for many years by governments of different political persuasions, and that would include recruitment and retention of sufficient clinicians. So a bad situation becomes acute when dealing with Covid.

Data for claims against care homes are hard to come by partly because on going litigation is not published and settled claims are not always revealed. NHS Resolution[25] publishes an annual report and accounts revealing the trends in claims, awards of damages by speciality and costs. This would not provide specific information about claims against care homes but makes interesting reading in the light of Covid. The annual report for the year ending 2021 reflects the first year of living with Covid to 31 March 2021; and it revealed that the liabilities decreased by £1.3 billion from the previous year, down from £84.1 billion to £82.8 billion with costs down by £120 million, to £2.26 billion. This was accompanied by an increase in claims of 951 to 12,629. They did state that they expected any claims arising from the pandemic to be made in future years. Even so they had set aside £500 million for Covid related claims. There were very few incident reports related to Covid in that year, which is not surprising. As NHSR comments, the average lag time between incident and notification (non-maternity) is 3.6 years so that year may not be representative of future litigation.

The net impact of Covid-19 cost £0.5 billion with a forecast to £1 billion for the next year. This reflected indirect impacts of Covid from delays, cancellations and misdiagnosis as a result of longer waiting lists.

In 2022/23 £2.64 billion was paid out which increased to £2.8 billion in 2023/24. Contrast this with 13,552 cases in the former year and

25 www.resolution.nhs.uk

13,382 in the latter. This last year also represented the year with the highest number of cases resolved pre-issue of proceedings at 81%.

The number of claims relating to Covid-19 was 22 in 2021/22 with only 7 in 2020/21. Clearly a very low number but one must appreciate that this records claims against the NHS and not against Care homes. Across the Clinical Negligence Scheme for Trusts, there was an increase in reported claims of 3.3% compared with 2021/22. This was a relatively modest increase and was still 1.7% lower than the average of the five years to 2019/20 preceding the pandemic. But numbers rose substantially by 8.6% in 2022/23, compared to the previous year. It could be surmised that as in clinical matters, law also experiences a backlog (in bringing claims) following Covid because of the inevitable operational challenges.

The majority of the financial provision set aside relates to maternity claims. In the annual report and accounts for 2023/24, obstetric claims accounted for the highest percentage at 13% of clinical claim numbers by volume but accounted for 57% of all clinical claims by value received. Another interesting statistic is the percentage of claims that are resolved by NHSR by the payment of damages– or as Claimants would describe it – the success rate which stood at 52%. This has been on a slightly increasing tide as 51% of cases prevailed in 2022/23 with 51.8% in 2021/22.

There has also been a rising tide of claims settled pre-issue of proceedings. 81% of claims settled pre-issue in 2023/24 against 80% in 2022/23.

So what does this mean for Claimants bringing or anticipating the commencement of a claim? Well, if a claim should be brought against an NHS Trust, NHS Resolution has set aside provision to settle meritorious cases. For those claims relating directly due to the treatment of Covid, £470 million has been allocated for damages and costs. For indirectly related claims such as delayed and misdiagnosis cases, especially cancer claims, £610 million has been set aside.

NHS Resolution launched the *Clinical Negligence Scheme for Coronavirus* that provided cover for Covid-19 claims not already covered by existing indemnity arrangements. It was established in accordance with the powers enabled by the *Coronavirus Act 2020*. The intention was to provide financial peace of mind and confidence to those clinicians undertaking NHS work to backfill others. For example where NHS Trusts were hosting special healthcare arrangements such as Nightingale hospitals then this indemnity arrangement applied. It also covered Local Authorities taking part in the Community Testing Programme.

There was a rare system of accord shown by lawyers practising clinical negligence during the pandemic. On 14 August 2020 a new protocol was finalised between NHS Resolution, the Society of Clinical Injury Lawyers (SCIL) and the charity, Action against Medical Accidents (AvMA). Known as the Covid-19 Clinical Negligence Protocol 2020. They agreed to suspend the usual limitation period of 3 years to bring a claim until three months after the protocol ended. It only applied to law firms that were members of AvMA or SCIL or any other organisation that was a signatory to the protocol. Therefore firms who were not party to the agreement or individual Claimants were bound by the usual limitation period and would be responsible for negotiating with the Defendant any extension of time to the limitation period. It remained in place until one of the parties gave notice to end it. Costs savings accompanied by a reduction in litigated claims of 6% in the financial years 2021 to 2023 were attributable (at least in part) to the protocol and this new détente in relations.

Such was its reported success that a revised Clinical Negligence Claims Agreement 2024 was developed and continued on from its predecessor. This is covered in Chapter 6 as it could almost be considered an adjunct to the Personal Injury and Clinical Disputes Protocol.

The deluge of cases that was anticipated does not appear to have transpired. The *Gardner* case had limited success for the Claimants and perhaps has led to a reality check for some law firms representing

Claimants. The judges concluded that the Department of Health March Discharge Policy and the April Admissions Guidance failed to recognise the risk to elderly and vulnerable residents from asymptomatic transmission. As such, those Government policies were irrational in that an asymptomatic patient discharged from hospital to a care home should be segregated from other residents for 14 days.

There have been reports in the media of cases brought under the ECHR following the loss of family members in care homes or hospital. 27 families reportedly had brought claims against the Secretary of State for health and social care alleging a breach of Articles 2,8 and 14 of the ECHR. The deaths occurred early in the pandemic from Covid-19. The Personal Representatives seek on behalf of the estates damages for loss of life, personal injuries, pain and suffering, anxiety, distress and feelings of injustice. Although detailed arguments are not known, it is expected that the claims will focus on failures to publish procedures, lack of appropriate guidance, policies and rules to be applied by residential care homes or nursing homes.

The current status of the litigation is unknown other than proceedings have been issued; that could be because there is a current stay to explore settlement or cases may have been disposed of on a without prejudice, confidential basis either by payment of damages and/or costs or they may have been discontinued. Given the publicity surrounding the cases, it is improbable that Claimants' families will go quietly and so litigation may be proceeding.

CHAPTER TWO

EVIDENCE AND RELEVANCE

2.1 INDEPENDENT INQUIRY

A Public Inquiry was set up by the former Conservative Government and chaired by Baroness Hallett, a retired judge of the Court of Appeal. This is independent of Government and has a broad remit to call witnesses, including then serving government ministers during the Covid-19 pandemic. Its principal role is to seek to learn from decisions made by the government and other relevant bodies such as the NHS and care sectors so that in the time honoured fashion lessons may be learnt so as to inform preparations for future pandemics across the UK.

A public inquiry under the *Inquiries Act 2005* arises where there are *'particular events have caused, or are capable of causing, public concern, or ...there is public concern that particular events may have occurred'.*

The Inquiry has been proceeding since June 2023 and is due to complete public hearings by summer 2026. Evidence revealed may be useful in pursuing a clinical negligence claim. But clearly that is a subsidiary issue when it is hoped that its recommendations are implemented. That will be politics.

Details of the Inquiry may be found at: *covid19.public-inquiry.uk*.

Although not a court of law, the Inquiry was established on a statutory basis with full powers under the *Inquiries Act 2005*. So the Chair has the power to compel the production of documents and to call witnesses to give evidence on oath. It is not adversarial although the Inquiry's Counsel, Hugo Keith KC has been rather effective at discovering inconsistencies and omissions.

It was tested by the government's attempts to avoid full disclosure such as diary records held by Boris Johnson, then Prime Minister and also from the Cabinet Office. The Cabinet Office launched a judicial review that was unsuccessful, the High Court holding that service of the s. 21 Inquiries Act 2005 notice was valid.

The Inquiry's remit was to examine, consider and report on preparations and the response to the pandemic across the UK up to the Inquiry's formal setting-up date, 28 June 2022. The Inquiry sets out its Terms of Reference. In short, the Inquiry is to hear evidence from politicians, civil servants, public health experts and bereaved families. Thereafter to consider the public health response; that of the health and care sectors; the economic response and its impact so as to identify the lessons learned that will inform preparations for future pandemics in the UK.

Structure

The Chair divided the Inquiry's investigation into modules. These are effectively separate phases examining specific areas:

- Module 1 – *Resilience and preparedness*
- Module 2 – *Care UK decision-making and political governance* (2A Scotland) (2B Wales) (2C Northern Ireland)
- Module 3 – *Impact of Covid-19 pandemic on healthcare systems in the 4 nations of the UK*
- Module 4 – *Vaccines and therapeutics*
- Module 5 – *Procurement*
- Module 6 – *Care sector*

- Module 7 – *Test, Trace and Isolate*
- Module 8 – *Children and Young People*
- Module 9 – *Economic response*
- Module 10 – *Impact on Society*

Each module has a preliminary hearing (which is procedural) and a full public hearing (hearing evidence from witnesses). As noted, there are 10 modules with some overlap of later preliminary hearings with earlier public hearings.

The first report was published on 18 July 2024 that covered Module 1 – *the United Kingdom's resilience and preparedness*. It contained 10 key recommendations. Baroness Hallett didn't pull her punches, finding that the UK was 'prepared for the wrong pandemic', was 'ill-prepared' and 'lacked resilience'. That much may not be too surprising to many people. There had been planning for an influenza outbreak but not for the global pandemic that ensued. The system of government with its many structures led to delegation, complex systems and inefficiency.

Risk assessment was flawed with too much reliance on a flu pandemic scenario; planning focused on dealing with the impact of the disease rather than prevention; a failure to appreciate long term risks and their effect on vulnerable people; the 2011 'UK influenza preparedness strategy' was not flexible enough to be adapted to use for Covid-19. It was commended for recognising the impact a pandemic would have and the three characteristics that would apply: capacity of healthcare, other public services and the behavioural response of the population to public health advice, antiviral medicines and use of healthcare services; the systems for test, trace and isolate were out dated and complex; there was a lack of broad scientific advice to Ministers who failed to challenge advice received; a lack of diverse perspectives leading to 'groupthink';

there were major omissions from the expert committees advising governments on pandemic preparedness.

The conclusion was that better preparedness for a pandemic would have avoided some financial and health cost. The UK must be better prepared in much the same way that we treat a threat from a hostile state.

Notably the former Health Secretary, Rt. Hon Matt Hancock criticised the government's preparedness for a pandemic, saying it was too focused on handling the aftermath of a pandemic rather than preventing one when resources were prioritised in the event of a no-deal Brexit. He stated that he *'didn't have the levers to act'* on adult social care as it was the responsibility of local authorities. He acknowledged that large-scale testing and contact tracing *'did not exist'* before Covid and that the UK lacked anti-viral treatments suitable for the pandemic.

The British Medical Association (BMA) which effectively is the Trades Union representing the interests of doctors, made submissions that were critical of the government. They considered that there were four key areas of deficiency in pandemic planning and resilience –

(i) a failure to ensure that doctors and healthcare workers were adequately protected when responding to a pandemic;

(ii) the lack of capacity and resources available;

(iii) a specific failure to ensure an adequate test and trace response; and

(iv) the government structures and processes were insufficient to address civil contingencies.

The BMA was concerned about the lack of appropriate PPE, both in volume and suitability. This was reinforced by other interested parties. They submitted that the government did not meet their responsibilities under health and safety law, including the provision of risk assessments. It was not until 24 June 2020, three months into the pandemic that NHS England issued a letter reminding employers to undertake risk assessments for their staff.

Module 2 examined political and administrative governance and decision-making. It included the initial response and central government decision-making. The Prime Minister together with the Health Secretary, Matt Hancock, the Secretary of State for Levelling Up, Housing and Communities, Michael Gove and the Chief Medical Officer for England and the Chief Scientific Officer, Chris Whitty and Patrick Vallance respectively were cross-examined by the Inquiry's Counsel.

The web of government departments and advisors is quite obtuse to the lay observer so the Inquiry produced an organogram (new to the author also). This depicted the chain of command and response structures.

This is a helpful module because it examines documents and evidence known to the government. Errors were made by the government; that much the former Prime Minister acknowledged, but could they have been avoided? It will be interesting to learn of the Chair's opinion when her report on Module 2 is published.

The Chief Medical Officer in giving evidence was critical of the lack of urgency akin to national security threats. On lockdown, he opined that the UK '*went a bit too late*' when lockdown was first implemented during the first wave of the pandemic. He gave four witness statements to the Inquiry. Asymptomatic spread of Covid-19 was a possibility and this is dealt with in his first statement.

Module 3 considered the impact of Covid on healthcare systems and core decision-making. The British Medical Association (BMA) believed that adequate protections were not put in place to protect staff from harm such as inadequate PPE, insufficient risk assessments and an initial lack of regular testing for staff and patients. Infection Prevention and Control guidance failed by failing to recognise that Covid-19 spreads via the air, leaving staff exposed and unprotected.

The findings of Module 3 and also Module 6 that examines the Care Sector will be especially appurtenant to lawyers and their clients in seeking to frame allegations of breach of duty relating to care homes.

Relevance

A public Inquiry does not find individuals or corporations liable for potentially criminal or negligent acts or omissions. But its findings may inform subsequent litigation.

Not everyone has been supportive of the Inquiry. Carl Heneghan, director of the University of Oxford's *Centre for Evidence-Based Medicine* gave evidence that the core issues of the pandemic had not been addressed and a failure to recognise the part to play for science. He believed that the side effects of '*Protect the NHS*' messaging reduced care for other diseases. He attacked the reliability of test-and-trace as well as the accuracy of epidemiological modelling in decision-making.

What will be crucial is whether Baroness Hallett's recommendations are implemented. However there is no requirement or obligation for a government to accept all or any of the inquiry's recommendations (as illustrated in the Leveson Inquiry). Given that there has been a change in government and that Labour are now in power (from 4 July 2024) with a substantial majority, one would expect implementation of all of the Chair's recommendations. Following the publishing of the first report, the Prime Minister, Sir Keir Starmer said the report confirmed that the UK had been underprepared for the pandemic and '*…that this government will learn the lessons from the inquiry*'. Time will tell if the recommendations are made on a timely basis. As Baroness Hallett has indicated that she wants to see changes in place within six months or a year. That would require the UK to implement a major overhaul of how the UK prepares for '*whole-system civil emergencies*' by July 2025, representing the first anniversary of her report on module 1. We shall see.

2.2 THE PARLIAMENTARY COMMITTEE REPORT

Select committees are cross-party non-partisan groups of MPs or Lords charged by parliament with a specific role or with investigating a specific issue. The intention is to hold the government to account. They can and do interact with and influence government legislation.

The House of Commons and Health and Social Care Committee and Science and Technology Committees reported on 12th October 2021 on the government's covid-19 pandemic response. It wasn't pretty. The Report, *Coronavirus: Lessons Learned to Date* revealed that unfortunately lessons have still not been learnt. Indeed the list of failures is long and dismal, describing the government's response as one of *'the most important public health failures the United Kingdom has ever experienced'*.

Those failures included the inadequate provision of PPE, hospital beds and ventilators and the management of Covid-19 within care homes.

The report may be found at https://committees.parliament.uk

It runs to 150 pages and contains 38 recommendations to the Government and public bodies. It drew on evidence from over 50 witnesses – including the then Health Secretary as well as Professor Chris Whitty and Sir Patrick Vallance.

The Report was agreed unanimously by members of both Select Committees, consisting of 22 MPs from the three main political parties. Their review began in October 2020 so just prior to the second lockdown in November 2020. Necessarily this was a contemporaneous investigation that could not know how the pandemic would play out.

The Committee examined six main areas:

- the country's pandemic preparedness;
- the use of border controls, social distancing and lockdowns to control the pandemic;
- the use of test, trace and isolate strategies;
- the impact of the pandemic on social care;
- the impact of the pandemic on specific communities; and
- the procurement and roll-out of covid-19 vaccines.

There were some positives but it mostly contained a critique of mistakes. It was hoped to provide a distillation of lessons as to how the UK could perform better in any new emergency. It found that Covid had resulted in more than 150,000 deaths in the UK, one of the highest per capita. The main points were:

- Social care was not given sufficient priority in the early stages of the pandemic. There were staff shortages, lack of sufficient testing and PPE. Buildings were poorly designed for isolation and infection control;
- The rapid discharge of elderly patients from hospitals to care homes without adequate testing or isolation was a mistake, leading to unnecessarily high deaths;
- Testing and contact tracing operations were *'slow, uncertain and chaotic'*. The delays in test, trace and isolate failed to contain the outbreak. Testing capacity should have been increased;
- Stopping community testing was mistaken;

- The initial decision to delay a comprehensive lockdown reflected fatalism. Other strategies such as isolation of infected individuals, robust border controls or effective test and trace should have been in place;

- The Government's early approach was akin to seeking herd immunity rather than to prevent the spread of Covid;

- The UK's preparedness for a pandemic was over-focused on a 'flu-model' which had not absorbed the lessons from SARS, MERS and Ebola. It performed les well than many other countries in practice;

- The NHS adapted to treating Covid patients, but continuity of care for other patients, such as cancer patients suffered.

The Committee examined the impact of Covid-19 on social care. They noted that before vaccination, the elderly were far more susceptible to die from Covid than younger people; those over 80 were 70 times more likely to die than 40 year olds and younger[26]. This much seems obvious and therefore the vulnerable were foreseeably at far greater risk of dying from Covid. So the arrangements to protect the elderly were of vast importance, especially during the early stages of the pandemic. Between 16 March 2020 and 30 April 2021, 41,675 care home residents died of covid-19 – nearly ¼ of all deaths[27]. And perturbingly during the pandemic (to October 2020), 74% of deaths recorded for social care workers had covid-19 recorded as a cause of death[28].

---

26 Public Health England, *'Disparities in the risk and outcomes of COVID-19'*, August 2020

27 Office for National Statistics, Deaths involving Covid-19 in the care sector, England and Wales: deaths occurring up to 12 June 2020

28 Public Health England, *'Disparities in the risks and outcomes of Covid-19'*, August 2020

Some of the witnesses considered that there was a lack of priority to social care during the initial phase of the pandemic. Professor David Oliver, a consultant geriatrician and Nuffield Trust fellow felt that 'Protect the NHS' meant protecting the acute hospital bed base with everything else being an afterthought.

The discharge of patients to care homes during the first wave of the pandemic reflected the prioritisation of the NHS over social care. Sir Simon Stevens, Chief Executive of NHS England instructed hospitals to urgently discharge all medically fit patients as soon as it was clinically safe to do so and care home residents were not tested on their discharge from hospital.

There was no expectation that patients would be Covid tested prior to discharge according to the Government's first set of guidance, issued on 19 March 2020[29]. This had the unintended consequence of contributing to the spread of infection in care homes. Seeding of infections also came about by staff entering care homes.

The report went on to say:

> *'Staff shortages, the lack of testing, difficulties in obtaining PPE and the design of care settings to enable communal living hampered isolation and infection control and the ability to keep Covid'.*

The Chair of the Health and Social Care Committee, the Rt Hon Jeremy Hunt MP (and a former Secretary of State for Health and Social Care) together with the Rt Hon Greg Clarke MP. Chair of the Science and Technology Committee (former Secretary of State for Business, Energy and Industrial Strategy) in a joint statement said:

> *'The UK response has combined some big achievements with some big mistakes. It is vital to learn from both to ensure that we perform as*

29 Gov.uk, COVID-19 Hospital Discharge Service Requirements, 19 March 2020

best we can during the remainder of the pandemic and in the future. Our vaccine programme was boldly planned and effectively executed. Our test and trace programme took too long to become effective. The Government took seriously scientific advice but there should have been more challenge from all to the early UK consensus that delayed a more comprehensive lockdown when countries like South Korea showed a different approach was possible'.

Significance

The conclusions and evidence of the Joint Committee was provided to the Public Inquiry into Covid-19. It will be noted that there is a degree of overlap between the Committee's investigation and the Inquiry. Importantly Baroness Hallett has reached similar conclusions with respect to preparedness (and will have heard similar evidence) about poor planning for the wrong pandemic. Health and social inequalities were exacerbated by the pandemic with the most vulnerable people exposed. There was a lack of attention to the systems that would help test, trace and isolate. They were both critical of '*groupthink*' whereby advisors tended to think about the same things in the same way.

Given that the Select Committee has concluded its enquiry and found multiple and significant errors by the then government in its handling of Covid, are the committee's findings and recommendations enforceable? Unfortunately not according to the Constitution Society[30]. There is no clear way in which enforcement or coercive powers could be exercised by Parliament or to impose sanctions. One could reflect on how Parliament would in effect seek to sanction the government, especially since there has been a change to Labour since the Committee reported. For our purposes, of more significance is whether the Courts will consider the findings. Because of Parliamentary privilege, which protects freedom of speech and debates or proceedings in parliament,

30 'Select Committees and coercive powers – clarity or confusion', pub 2012 www.consoc.org.uk

the courts hitherto have not involved themselves in proceedings in Parliament. It cannot be persuasive but evidence given and findings made may have some beneficial value.

2.3 INQUEST

An inquest can bring some beneficial evidence into the forum for a civil claim and provide limited opportunities for families to hear from witnesses, possibly medical experts and to ask non-leading questions. The purpose of an inquest is to establish facts, namely:

- identity of the deceased
- when, where and how the death occurred
- the facts required to report to the Registrar of births, deaths and marriages.

It is not to attribute blame or seek findings of negligence.

A Coroner will usually require a Post Mortem ('PM') to establish medical cause of death before deciding if an inquest is necessary. A PM may encompass a full/partial body dissection or could be non-invasive and may simply require examination of the body and possibly taking of bodily samples or fluids or MRI scanning. They may list for a pre-inquest review.

Verdicts are limited and may be natural causes; accident or misadventure; suicide; unlawful killing; alcohol; drug related; industrial disease; Road traffic collision; neglect; open (insufficient evidence as to how death came about; and narrative (with brief circumstances as to cause of death).

The Coroner may combine some of these conclusions and may provide a report at the end of the inquest.

Our interest is whether the death was caused or contributed to by Covid-19 or some other disease where there was a delay in diagnosis and treatment during and post pandemic. Did death result from neglect in a Care home?

On 26 March 2020, the Chief Coroner published guidance no. 34 for the approach to be adopted for all Coroners in England and Wales on the approach to be taken to Covid-19. Various updates took place, including no. 37 addressing possible exposure in the workplace.

Not all Covid deaths will be or have been reported to the Coroner. At the time of the pandemic, medical practitioners certifying death were governed by the requirements under the *Notification of Deaths Regulations* 2019 ('NDR') *The* Ministry of Justice published its interim guidance that stated:

> *'Whilst Covid-19 is a notifiable disease under the Health Protection (Notification) Regulations 2010, a death caused by Covid-19 virus is not reason of its own to notify the death to the coroner'.*

Covid-19 is considered a naturally occurring disease and is therefore capable of being a natural cause of death according to the Chief Coroner. As such it does not require investigation by the Coroner and should be dealt with via the Medical Certificate Cause of Death ('MCCD') process unless there is some additional factor at play.

The *Coronavirus Act 2020* (CA) section 30 was introduced to moderate the workload of Coroners by amending the notifiable provision. Covid-19 now was not a notifiable disease such that if an inquest was opened into a death involving Covid-19, no jury was required. The Coroner however retained discretion to do so where appropriate.

The CA allowed any registered medical practitioner to sign an MCCD, even where the deceased was not attended to in their last illness, provided that the doctor could state the cause of death to the best of their knowledge and belief. This easement expired on 24 March 2022. Even without diagnostic proof such as a positive test for Covid, if the person had symptoms typical of Covid-19 infection, it was acceptable to give Covid-19 as the cause of death.

Regulation 3 of the NDR sets out the circumstances when a notification to the Coroner should be made. In cases involving care homes, situations that may be relevant are: use of a medicinal product or controlled drug; a disease attributable to employment; neglect; an unnatural death; unknown cause of death; no attending practitioner was available within a reasonable time.

There are instances in which a Covid-19 death may be reported to the Coroner, such as where the virus has been contracted in a workplace, such as a hospital or care home. A Coroner must investigate a death where there is reason to suspect that it was unnatural, such as where it resulted from the effects of a naturally occurring condition or disease, e.g. Covid-19 but where some human error contributed to death. So where there is human failure that contributed to infection or death from Covid-19 then an investigation may be required. An example may be inadequate provision of PPE for clinicians in a particular care home. It would not, however, be appropriate to investigate the adequacy of general policies of PPE in the UK or as a result of NHS guidance.

Defendants may dispute that death was caused by Covid-19, particularly where the deceased had an underlying condition or they argue that it was not contracted in a care home or hospital but rather the community. This may be raised at a pre-inquest review if they should dispute the need for an inquest. The Coroner is not constrained by law nor policy and has a wide ambit of discretion. If there is 'reason to suspect' that the deceased died an unnatural death because of human failure then an inquest is indicated. If MCCD is Covid-19 or a contribution and the location is a Care home or at least possible exposure was contracted there, then one would expect the Coroner to proceed to an inquest.

The Coroner may not be aware of a death, perhaps because it was not reportable under *Reporting of Injuries, Diseases and Dangerous Occurrences Regulations 2013* (RIDDOR) to the HSE. This applies to death as a result of occupational exposure to a biological agent – including the virus that causes Covid-19. Since 1 April 2022, revised guidance on reporting to RIDDOR applied, requiring cases where someone was incidentally exposed to Covid such as in the health and social care sectors to make a report, i.e. death was not a prerequisite.

There is contact between Coroners and the HSE. A situation could arise whereby an employee infected a family member with Covid, from which they died. This would not be reportable and hence the Coroner would not be aware. Reliance would then be on family to contact the Coroner or via perhaps a GP or local Solicitor.

2.4 EXPERT EVIDENCE

Specialism. In order to prove breach of duty and causation, expert evidence will be necessary. The Pre-Action Protocol for the Resolution of Clinical Disputes (paragraph 4.1) provides that expert opinions may be needed –

- On breach of duty;
- On causation;
- On the patient's condition and prognosis;
- To assist in valuing aspects of the claim.

The type of expert depends on the alleged breach and injury caused. So a Claimant who has contracted Covid-19 will have to establish where and how they were infected. In a fatality, did Covid cause or materially contribute to the cause of death? Experts on breach could be from Nurse Practitioners, Geriatricians, Physicians; on causation from Microbiologists, Virologists, Statisticians, Immunologists, Occupational health & safety experts and Epidemiologists for example. That is a lot of experts. Experts could go beyond those mentioned if one is exploring a delay case, for example where contracting Covid caused a delay in undergoing treatment, or delay existed because of the pandemic. If a patient had to wait for investigations into suspected cancer with resultant delays in treatment, then experts may be necessary in Oncology and Oncological surgery.

The standard of care will be different during Covid times and is likely to be judged less harshly, making the Claimants' task more onerous. With a constraint on resources both financial and with a reduced availability of clinicians contending with Covid cases, prioritisation (which has always existed) becomes more acute. Patients who otherwise would have been examined in the surgery or in hospital may have had a virtual appointment via Zoom or Teams. Diseases may have been missed as a result. Waiting times may have been extended.

One of the crucial questions that will need to be posed to a breach expert is what was a reasonable practice during Covid-times. Necessarily this will require close examination as to the state of knowledge about Covid, its transmissibility and guidance provided by the government and Care home policies at a particular time. This is likely to change as the pandemic evolved and with that comes altered advice and clinical practices. So an expert must not only be expert in their particular speciality, but also be alive to changes during Covid and how that may impact on reasonable standards of care. So one could foresee that a Defendant may rely upon the limited state of knowledge at the beginning of the pandemic in March 2020, should an alleged breach refer to that period as being more excusable, and therefore not actionable, than if it occurred during the third wave when procedures and protocols should have been more refined.

Expert evidence is important in proving statutory duty since strict liability was removed following the *Enterprise and Regulatory Reform Act 2013.* Evidence of best practice or at least accepted practice will be necessary and whether sufficient steps had been taken to ensure the safety of employees. Pre-action disclosure of Risk assessments should be sought as well as health and safety material. Guidance on risk assessments may be obtained from www.hse.gov.uk/risk/controlling-risks/.

Choosing your expert. Getting the right expert is critical in proving the claim and succeeding. Established solicitors will maintain a database of 'tried and tested' experts. But they may not necessarily be expert in issues surrounding Covid. Indeed few would be unless they have been practising 'in the thick of it'. And that is key; they must have relevant experience and ideally still be active in clinical practice. If the claim is against a private care home provider then someone from that background is necessary, rather than someone from a teaching hospital, for example; preferably has had previous experience as an expert witness; not treated the Claimant nor worked nor had any professional relationship with the Defendant that may present a conflict of interest or potential conflict. Their CV should be carefully scrutinised to demonstrate sufficient knowledge and experience. Whilst it will be difficult to discern from a CV, the expert must demonstrate credibility and a robust demeanour (but not one that is inflexible). By which we mean that should the Claimant's expert happen to know any of the Defendant's experts, they will not feel obliged to be subservient to one who may once have been their senior or mentor. You do not wish to learn following a joint meeting of experts that your expert agrees with his counterpart as he always agrees with him. An initial telephone discussion with a new expert may be helpful to try and gauge their approach and previous experience of cases that have gone to trial or been abandoned. One of the tactics Defendants may employ is to challenge the credentials of experts, so researching their background is important. The breach expert will need to come from the same specialism where sub-standard care is alleged. In cases where the procedures for safeguarding against Covid are challenged, one must determine who devised those policies and who was responsible for their implementation. Nursing care is likely to feature predominantly. There are some excellent medico-legal agencies that will be able to advise on suitability for the inexperienced legal practitioner.

Instructing the expert. Instructions to experts should clarify the nature of your instructions and their duties as an expert under Part 35 of the Civil Procedure Rules. The relevant test under *Bolam* and *Bolitho* for breach should be provided. It is not unheard of for a breach medical expert to stray into condition & prognosis unless absolute clarity is given detailing their remit. A summary of the facts is helpful and the evidence distilled from the witness statements. A detailed chronology of the evolution of the pandemic with particular emphasis on infection control measures may be necessary. Witness statements from the Claimant addressing the care home's procedures alone are unlikely to be sufficient, though any written guidance may be appended to their statement. It may require an expert in public health or in statistics. The expert may need to address evolution of the pandemic, the state of knowledge at a particular time and guidance given and implemented. More than any other time, it will assist the Court more effectively if the expert is practising as a clinician and can testify to the pressures and priorities (where they apply) during Covid times. It has been acceptable hitherto to have experts who are retired but kept abreast of clinical practice. That applies less so where the pandemic applies.

A paginated bundle of medical and care records should accompany the instructions, together with witness statements and a chronology. If the breach expert is reporting on procedures rather than injury and causation, they may not require GP records. However they may be relevant to identify vulnerabilities. If in doubt send them all.

There may be questions to ask of the expert arising from perusal of the records or the information set out in statements. One should not be dictatorial in how an expert chooses to lay out their report but they may be asked to address:

- A summary of relevant care/nursing records, advising on the quality of care and where this departed from reasonable and responsible care in accordance with accepted practice, with references or exhibits. Did this constitute a breach of duty in accordance with the Bolam standard? (if a breach report).

- A summary of all relevant medical records on history, condition and prognosis, detailing any exacerbation of condition, impact on life expectancy (for a condition report). Reference should be made to the Claimant's statement identifying any disablement and quality of life issues directly caused by Covid.

- A summary of all relevant medical records advising on pre-existing health conditions/co-morbidities and opinion on how the Claimant's condition would have been different had appropriate care been provided. Has there condition been caused or materially contributed to by breach of duty (for the report on medical causation).

- A supplemental report may be necessary for the condition expert to comment on the Claimant's schedule of loss and whether such is reasonable and necessary as a result of their condition caused by breach of duty. They should make reference to the Claimant's statement.

- If the expert has any concerns about the case, for example any inconsistencies in the Claimant's evidence or medical records, they should be advised, at least initially, to include this in a side letter rather than their report. It may be that there is an innocent explanation or it may not be relevant to the enquiry. Ultimately if it is relevant to their instructions and their opinion, then it must go in the report consistent with the expert's duty to the court.

- The expert should be asked whether any additional evidence or documents may assist them or the claim more generally. If the expert is uncertain of their remit or relevance then they should be encouraged to contact their instructing lawyer. It would be rare to have an initial conference with the expert before preparing their draft report. It may be that following receipt that a conference with solicitor and counsel is desirable before the report is finalised.

It is all very well advocating for the use of many experts in various disciplines (as the author has just done) but they will need to be paid for and the Court's permission granted at a Case Management Conference. One can anticipate resistance from Defendants and perhaps from District judges mindful of cost budgets with concerns about proportionality. The trend appears to be for less rather than more experts. But ultimately Claimants must be allowed the opportunity to prove their case and justiciability, it is suggested, should trump other considerations. There is further discussion about this in chapter 6 about case management post issue of proceedings.

2.5 SCHEDULE OF LOSS

The restitution of damages could fill an entire textbook on the subject ('McGregor on Damages anyone?) so this is an attempt to give a brief flavour of items to consider in forming part of the claim.

A Schedule of (financial) loss ('SOL'), or special damages is strictly not evidence but it is a document that needs to be proved and forms a vital part of the claim that requires early consideration. The principle of damages is to ensure that the Claimant is reimbursed for their or their families' financial outlay caused by negligence and to restore them wherever possible to the position had there been no negligence. That is really a fiction because one cannot roll back time pre-injury but the intention is compensatory to reflect the injury and no more.

The Courts expect that details are provided early on in the case and if possible should accompany the Letter of Claim ('LOC'). Given that the Claimant may wish to make a Part 36 offer with the LOC, a fully particularised schedule is essential if all heads of loss are to be recovered. They comprise general damages representing pain, suffering and loss of amenity for the injury sustained (physical and mental) and other intangible losses such as loss of leisure or sociability. The second limb are special damages comprising the actual and future financial losses incurred and to be incurred. Although the assessment of general damages is one for the court to determine, conventionally reference is made in the SOL to medical evidence on condition and prognosis as well as case authorities (for similar injuries) and the Judicial College Guidelines that provides a general tariff on general damages.

Typically a SOL format would divide the specials into past financial losses that have been incurred already and for which there may be documentary evidence of expenditure, such as invoices, purchase notes and receipts. Such pecuniary losses for a care home resident may include such mundane items as: toiletries, clothing, travel (including those of family and friends) to significant expenditure that has been incurred such as private medical treatment, additional care costs, a portable ventilator or other equipment; and any loss of earnings incurred by a relative in taking time off to visit or provide care and respite to the Claimant. Time spent in providing care and assistance is potentially recoverable where it is reasonable and necessary. There may be some overlap and potential for duplication with professional nursing care so this is a head that is likely to be challenged. Although it does not come naturally, those expending time in helping or visiting the Claimant should keep a diary to record what they have done. Witness statements will be necessary from them to prove this aspect of the claim.

Future pecuniary losses are clearly more difficult to calculate as there are various imponderables and assumptions that have to be made, often with the benefit of medical evidence in support. One starts with the actual cost of the item (known as the multiplicand). So in a claim for future care, that may be worked up by ascertaining an hourly rate. For gratuitous care provided by a family member, the rate is less than a professional carer but that may be the starting point by examining the cost from local government National Joint Council wages and deducting say 25%. The hours spent over say a week are then determined and that is the notional cost. The issue then is for how long is that care required, bearing in mind that care was necessary anyway and becomes more necessary as the Claimant ages. This is known as the multiplier and is discounted to reflect life's exigencies and the fact that receipt of a lump sum may be invested to achieve a return. Actuarial tables known as the Ogden tables are used to determine the multiplier. So in simple terms if a Claimant will never recover from their injuries caused by negligence, their future losses will be calculated up until their anticipated death. The multiplier will be less than the number of years left so to speak but much depends on various factors, not least their age and health.

It becomes more difficult in the case of a fatality where there are dependants. This begs two questions. Firstly is there a dependency and who is entitled in law to be a dependant? Dealing with the class of dependants. Under the *Fatal Accidents Act 1976* a dependant is a spouse; civil partner; parent; grandparent; child or child of the family (step-child); sibling; aunt or uncle; and any person who was living with the deceased for at least two years as if they were husband and wife/civil partner. The last category of person really applies to co-habiting partners. In order to be successful in a claim for loss of financial dependency, the Claimant must show that they had received financial support in the past, or that they had a reasonable expectation that they would be supported financially in the future. The breakdown of a relationship is not necessarily a bar to financial dependency.

To calculate financial dependency, start with the deceased's net financial contribution to the home. For someone who was an elderly resident in a care home, financial dependency is more likely to represent gifts of money to a relative rather than contribution towards household expenses. However, for a younger deceased person who perhaps was resident for respite care or was an employee, the claim may reflect their loss of earnings and services. If the deceased had young children, they may have lost their primary carer and so a claim for loss of future services should be made. In such a scenario, another relative would be expected to step in to care for a child. It may be that there was co-parenting, sharing childcare responsibilities and now the sole parent must undertake all child rearing. Have they had to give up work or go part-time? Does another relative assist? Howsoever this terrible dilemma is resolved, there is either a claim for future loss of earnings dependency for the surviving parent or a claim for lost services. There is case authority to suggest that such care is provided at a commercial rate with no discount to reflect the special nature of the lost service.

In a claim for loss of earnings, the conventional approach is to add both spouses' incomes together and deduct 25% where there is one or more children, or a deduction of 34% if no children. From that is subtracted the Claimant's residual earnings capacity. This provides the annual multiplicand. The multiplier must then be calculated in a similar manner to that for services using the Ogden tables. The period between death and trial is treated as a past loss and so future losses start from the notional date of trial. This approach may vary according to the financial circumstances so should be treated as a 'rule of thumb'.

In addition the Courts will make a separate award for the intangible loss of a parent's love and affection. The award is in the discretion of the court and may vary from nil to a sum exceeding £10,000.00.

In addition to a possible dependency, Claimants may recover funeral expenses and possibly damages for bereavement, though eligibility is more restricted than for dependency. Current eligibility is for a spouse or civil partner of the deceased, cohabiting partners and parents (if the deceased was 'legitimate', unmarried and a minor), or the mother only (if the deceased was 'illegitimate', unmarried and a minor). The statutory payment under the *Fatal Accidents Act* is £15,120.00 (from 1 May 2020).

The extent of the claim and whether there is a financial dependency will reflect complexity. It would be unusual in a care claim for a large specials claim. In that event, one may wish to run past counsel before disclosing to the Defendant. It is always easier to revise downwards than upwards.

CHAPTER THREE

CASE LAW

3.1 GARDNER

In May 2020 when some 20,000 care home residents had died of Covid-19, two daughters whose fathers (Michael Gibson and Donald Percival Maynard Harris) had also died from Covid-19, brought claims in the Administrative division of the High Court for breach of human rights under Article 2 and Article 8 ECHR and for judicial review. The Claimants sought declarations that particular policies of the Defendants (the Health Secretary, NHS England and Public Health England) constituted breaches of their fathers' rights under the European Convention on Human Rights, or alternatively were unlawful and susceptible to judicial review under the common law. The Claimants did not claim compensation, but sought appropriate declarations by the court.

That case was:

R (on the application) of (1) Dr Cathy Gardner (2) Ms Fay Harris v (1) Secretary of State for Health and Social Care (2) NHS Commissioning Boards (NHS England) (3) Public Health England [2022] EWHC 967 (Admin).

The High Court held unanimously that the arrangements by the Department of Health for discharging patients from hospitals to care homes during the pandemic were unlawful. As such, the Claimants' common law claim against the Secretary of State and Public Health England (the 1st and 3rd Defendant) was upheld in part while their human rights claim failed. The claims against the 2nd Defendant failed.

The case concerned a challenge to four policies that resulted in Covid-19 positive individuals being transferred from hospitals into care homes and then infecting residents. The four policies were issued between 13 March and 15 April 2020. The Claimants alleged that the Government was slow to act on the growing consensus of asymptomatic transmission; asymptomatic patients were transferred to care homes when it was already known about the risks of community transmission.

The four policies

1) *'Guidance: Coronavirus (COVID-19) – Guidance on Residential Care Provision – Public Health England'*, referred to in the proceedings as 'The March PHE Policy', issued on 13 March 2020 and remained in force until 6 April 2020.

2) A combination of '*Next Steps on NHS Response to COVID-19'*, dated 17 March 2020 ('the March NHSE Instruction'), and *'COVID-19 Hospital Discharge Service Requirements'*, dated 19 March 2020 ('the March Discharge Requirements'). This policy remained extant until 15 April 2020.

3) *'Admission and Care of Patients During COVID-19 Incident in a Care Home'*, dated 2 April 2020 ('the April Admissions Guidance').

4) *'COVID-19: Our Action Plan for Adult Social care'*, dated 15 April 2020 ('the April Action Plan').

The first policy was challenged on the basis that it failed to address the risk from visitors to care homes and effectively caused infection to 'seed' into care homes when the government considered that community transmission had been occurring for 2 weeks. The guidance stated that care home providers reviewed their own policies to ensure that no one who was suspected of COVID-19 or was generally unwell should visit care homes. But it did not address those who were infected with COVID-19 but did not have symptoms. On this advice, such visits could continue. It was argued that the policy not only failed to address the risk of transmission from staff but actually increased it.

The Claimants also challenged the guidance on personal protective equipment ('PPE') that stated that if neither the individual receiving care had symptoms, then PPE was not required above normal good hygiene. Yet there was contradiction with the Guidance for infection prevention and control in healthcare settings ('the March NHS Guidance') that advised that PPE should always be worn by all healthcare workers. The policy also failed to address the risks arising from use of agency and bank staff. The March PHE policy encouraged the sharing of workforce between providers, thus inviting an increase in staff working across multiple facilities which increased infection risk.

In addition the Claimants assert that the policy failed to address the risk of transmission from other residents, especially those being newly admitted or re-admitted. Further, there was no testing, isolation or instruction to use PPE. This, despite SAGE's conclusion on 10 March 2020 that community transmission was underway. Finally, they argue that the policy failed to provide adequate guidance on infection control measures to be adopted in care homes.

In the Defendants' rebuttal of the March PHE Policy, they argued a belief that 'transmission occurred from symptomatic individuals' and pointed to concerns about *'potential physical and emotional impacts on residents and their families'* if visits were completely restricted.

Staffing levels were maintained to alleviate pressure on numbers. As regards visitors, the Defendants relied on the same Policy advising anyone with COVID-19 symptoms not to visit a care home. They submitted that the first case of COVID in a care home was detected on 10 March 2020, with formal restrictions introduced on 2 April 2020. Prior to that, care homes were asked to review their visiting policy which the Defendants contended was a reasonable approach. In any event, they went on to assert that early studies found that allowing visitors into care homes had only a marginal impact.

The second policy challenged by the Claimants was termed the 'March Discharge Policy'. It referred to documents entitled '*Next Steps on NHS Response to COVID-19*' dated 17 March 2020, and '*COVID-19 Hospital Discharge Service Requirements*', dated 19 March 2020. It was contended by the Claimants that this caused a large transfer of infected hospital patients into care homes (containing the most vulnerable) without testing, isolation or guidance about PPE or whether the care home could provide safe care. The argument went that this policy prioritised hospital bed capacity rather than safety of care home residents. And that a failure to provide testing was not justifiable nor to recommend isolation given the Government's self-isolation policy; namely that a COVID-19 positive case had to self-isolate for 14 days.

The Defendants opposed this complaint by relying on policy guidance to clinicians to decide whether a COVID-19 test was appropriate for patients during their hospital stay. Individual assessments would be undertaken to ascertain whether it was safe to discharge with the aim to free up NHS facilities for the most severely affected cases. In any event, they argued that testing and isolation for discharges was introduced four weeks later. During that time, capacity increased from 2,100 tests on 1 March 2020 to 38,766 tests, explained by practical constraints and scientific advice.

Mandatory isolation was introduced in April 2020 when new scientific advice emerged but prior to that, the Defendants maintained that benefits had to be weighed against harms of isolating vulnerable people and feasibility of agreeing a nationwide policy was not feasible. Ultimately it was down to each care home and local authorities to exercise individual risk assessments to ensure sufficient safeguards. This does sound like abrogating responsibility.

The Third Policy had the title '*Admission and Care of Patients During COVID-19 Incident in a Care Home*' and dated 2 April 2020. This attracted a similar claim to the second Policy in that the guidance failed to protect care home residents and prioritised the Defendants' objective of freeing up hospital beds. Negative tests were still not required before discharge into care homes. Strangely there was no distinction between asymptomatic individuals and those who had tested positive -but no longer showing symptoms- when it came to delivery of their care. Staff should only wear PPE around residents with symptoms. Visitors were discouraged from attending care homes rather than prohibited.

The Defendants repeated their response to that stated previously addressing testing, isolation, hospital beds and asymptomatic individuals. Testing started for symptomatic staff on 15 April 2020 while asymptomatic staff became eligible on 28 April 2020. A PPE hotline was developed for care homes by 16 March 2020. This author is unsure what that could have achieved. Restrictions on staff transfers between care homes was said to be very difficult reflecting the structure of the care sector and the necessity to avoid staff shortages.

The fourth Policy appeared to reverse previous policies requiring testing of all patients discharged to care homes from hospital. This was called the *'COVID-19: Our Action Plan for Adult Social Care'*, known in the proceedings as the April Action Plan (and dated 15 April 2020). It was suggested –though not mandatory- that individuals from the community may be isolated for 14 days. Although an improvement on previous practices, the Claimants disputed the Defendants' claim that the advice changed due to new cogent evidence regarding the risks of asymptomatic transmission. The Claimants remained critical about the delay in testing and no restrictions on staff movement implemented or isolation of residents from the community.

The Defendants

There were three Defendants named in the proceedings.

The First Defendant was the Secretary of State for Health and Social Care. This office has responsibility for policy in the field of adult social care in England. At the material time between 9 July 2018 to 26 June 2021, the office was held by the Rt. Hon Matt Hancock MP.

The Second Defendant was the NHS Commissioning Board; often known as NHS England. This is a statutory corporation with its own Board.

The Third Defendant was Public Health England. The First Defendant is responsible in law for the Third Defendant.

The court was advised that some 97% of care homes in England are not operated by any of the Defendants in *Gardner*. So this was a public law claim and did not involve private care homes as Defendants – nor in fact any care homes outside the private sector. That said, the court reminded itself that the First Defendant has the power under s 20 of the health and Social Care Act 2008 to regulate care homes so as to cause no 'avoidable harm'.

During the first wave of the pandemic, no new regulations were introduced. So while the Defendants had the power of persuasion and guidance, they had no power in law to require care homes to admit patients, nor to require them to remain open.

<u>The Common law claim</u>

The claim was formulated under the Equality Act 2010 – sections 19, 29 and 149. Only s 149 (the Public Sector Equality Duty, PSED) was pursued to trial.

This imposes an obligation to have regard to the need to (a) eliminate discrimination, harassment, victimisation and any other conduct prohibited under the Act; (b) advance equality of opportunities to those who share a protected characteristic or who do not share it; (c) foster good relations to those who share a protected characteristic or who do not share it.

The court did not devote considerable time in determining this part of the claim. The Government could not reasonably be criticised for failing to carry out an equalities impact assessment of its policies relating to care homes addressing the need to eliminate discrimination against the elderly or the need to advance equality of opportunity between the elderly and the rest of the population. They held that the PSED did not add anything to the Defendants' duties at common law. Any policy affecting care homes would reflect the fact that the majority of such residents would be elderly with other health issues making them particularly vulnerable to infections, whether s 149 had been enacted or not.

The human rights claim

Initially the claim was brought under Articles 2,3,8 and 14 of the European Convention on Human Rights (ECHR). Articles 3 and 14 were subsequently dropped and not pursued at trial. The court held that the Defendants did not owe the Article 2 operational duty and that there was no breach of the 'systems duty'.

Article 2 of the ECHR enshrines the right to life, requiring states to instigate various operational and systemic duties. The 'systemic duty' requires appropriate legislative and administrative frameworks to be put in place to protect the right to life. The court was satisfied that the government had provided guidance that constituted frameworks.

It was accepted by all parties that the Claimants did not need to prove causation; they did not need to prove on the balance of probabilities that the deceased died as a result of actions or omissions by the Defendants. For the purposes of the ECHR claim, the Claimants had to show that care home residents were put at greater risk of harm as a result of the actions and inactions complained about, i.e. an increased risk to life. That matter was settled as the (then) most recent and authoritative study showed that the discharge of hospital patients into care homes did put residents at significantly greater risk.

The Systems duty

The systems duty requires the State to have a regulatory framework in place designed to provide effective measures to protect life. The Court agreed with Defence Counsel that this amounted to a '*high level structural* duty'.

The Claimants referred to <u>*Kolyadenko v Russia*</u> [2013] 56 EHRR 2, a case about flooding from a reservoir. The court found that there was a positive obligation to have a legislative and administrative framework in place to provide effective deterrence against threats to life, including practical measures to ensure effective protection of citizens whose lives might be endangered. It was submitted by extension that the duty applied in the context of any activity in which the right to life might be at stake. And here the activity was the operation and regulation by the State of care homes caring for vulnerable people. The virus created such a risk of magnitude that the State through regulation and intervention was obliged to act against to ensure protection of care home residents.

Another case against Russia was also relied upon by the Claimants, namely <u>*Budayeva v Russia*</u> (2014) 59 EHRR 2 which was another case in which the Article 2 duty was engaged and breached. The court examined practical measures that the State had taken to protect against mudslides, said to create a foreseeable, mortal risk to residents.

Therefore it was submitted that Article 2 did require the Government to protect the population from a serious threat to life and especially the uniquely vulnerable care home population, whose treatment was heavily regulated by the State. Furthermore, it was suggested that this was not only a positive obligations case like the aforementioned cases, but rather one where the Defendants had actually taken actions which increased the risk to life; for example, the Discharge Policy and the April Admissions Guidance seeking to give reassurance to care homes to admit new residents, as well as encouragement of staff sharing.

The Court considered the case of *Fernandes de Oliveira v Portugal*, 31 January 2019 that concerned allegations of medical negligence in the context of the suicide of an inpatient in a psychiatric hospital who escaped the premises and jumped in front of a train. The hospital had been aware of his previous suicide attempts. The Grand Chamber of the ECHR said that in the context of healthcare, the State must *'make regulations compelling hospitals, whether private or public, to adopt appropriate measures for the protection of patients' lives'.* The ECHR went on to find that the question as to whether there has been a failure by the State to comply with its regulatory duties calls for a concrete rather than an abstract assessment of any alleged deficiency.

In short work, the Court held that there was no arguable case that the systems duty had been breached. There was nothing wrong with the framework for the issuing of guidance or policy documents by the Defendants.

The Operational duty

The parties agreed that three key factors must be present for the Article 2 operational duty to apply:

(1) a real and immediate risk to life;

(2) actual or constructive knowledge of the State of the risk;

(3) a sufficient connection or link with the responsibility of the State ('the *Rabone* criteria' – see below).

The Claimants relied upon the case of *Rabone v Pennine Care NHS Foundation Trust* [2012] UKSC 2. This concerned a voluntary psychiatric patient who committed suicide having been allowed to leave hospital when she was at real and immediate risk of death by suicide. The claim was against the NHS Trust said to be responsible, in part under Article 2. The court held there was an escalating 5%-20% risk of suicide to be a sufficiently real risk.

Lord Dyson in *Rabone* recited the three distinct duties imposed upon the State to protect life, namely: (i) a negative duty to refrain from taking life, save in exceptional circumstances; (ii) a positive duty to conduct a proper and open investigation into deaths for which the State might be responsible; and (iii) a positive duty to protect life in certain circumstances.

It was the latter duty to protect life with which the Court was concerned. That involves two elements, set out in *Osman v United Kingdom* (2000) 29 EHRR 245. The first is a general duty on the State 'to put in place a legislative and administrative framework designed to provide effective deterrence against threats to the right to life'. The second is what has been called the 'operational duty'.

In *Osman* the ECHR found that Article 2 may imply *in certain well-defined circumstances* a positive obligation on the authorities to take preventative operational measures to protect an individual whose life is at risk from the criminal acts of another individual. In the present case, the Court observed that the circumstances imposing the Article 2 operational duty are 'well-defined' a quarter of a century later. Baroness Hale in *Rabone* stated that the court's tendency is to state the principle in very broad terms, without defining the circumstances in which it will apply.

Lord Dyson in *Rabone* found that the ECHR has expanded the circumstances in which the operational duty is owed, so as to include dangers for which the State is responsible. He considered the decision in *Powell v United Kingdom* (2000) 30 EHRR CD 62 to help discover the 'essential features' of cases where Strasbourg had recognised the existence of an operational duty. The existence of a 'real and immediate risk' to life is a necessary but not sufficient condition for the existence of the duty. As the Court of Appeal has said, a patient undergoing major surgery may be facing a real and immediate risk of death and yet

Powell shows that there is no article 2 operational duty to take reasonable steps to avoid the death of such a patient.

Lord Dyson was not able to elicit any criteria from ECHR decisions to determine whether an article 2 operational duty exists in any particular circumstances. Therefore an examination of cases was necessary to determine why the operational duty existed in some circumstances and not in others. The paradigm example where there was an assumption of responsibility by the State for an individual's welfare and safety applied where the State had detained an individual, whether in prison, in a psychiatric hospital or an immigration detention centre, for example.

When the article 2 operational duty has been breached, the vulnerability of the victim is a relevant consideration, to such a degree that on occasions, no assumption of control was necessary. The level of risk is also a factor.

The Defendants were critical of the Claimants' reference to cases such as *Kolyadenko, Stoicescu* etc. when those cases had specific features. The closest cases to the present context were said to be *R (Maguire) v HM Senior Coroner for Blackpool* [2021] QB 409 and *R (Morahan) v West London Assistant Coroner* [2021] QB 1205 which were about alleged medical negligence in care settings. In *Maguire,* Defence Counsel examined the Court of Appeal's judgment to break down ECHR case law into three broad categories of cases in the context of health and social care. In cases involving alleged medical negligence of a patient's care in the care home, the State's obligations were primarily regulatory in nature. Thus it was a duty to take necessary measures to ensure implementation, including supervision and enforcement. In the context of medical negligence, State responsibility arises in only very exceptional circumstances such as when a patient's life has knowingly been put at risk by denial of emergency treatment.

The Defendants submitted that the present case was not within any of the established categories where the operational duty was held to arise in a health and social care context. It was not a medical treatment case, nor a denial of life saving treatment case, nor an institutional case where the State was responsible for giving rise to the conditions creating the risk to life. Most care home residents were not under the control of the State at all.

They further argued that there was no relevant State responsibility triggering the operational duty in this case. Though the Government had put in place Covid policies to assist in the treatment and care of those in care homes did not supply the necessary element of State responsibility. Furthermore, while the care sector was regulated, that did not mean that care residents were controlled by the State. Defence Counsel also compared to a medical negligence case, suggesting it would be incoherent to subject the State to stricter controls when managing the virus that threatened the entire population than when it was managing individual medical negligence cases.

Here, the court reflected on the environmental cases cited by the Claimants that concerned failures by municipal authorities to take any steps to mitigate a physical threat to inhabitants in a particular locality. But the Court found that such cases could not be relied upon to found an Article 2 operational duty to the entire population of any member state to protect it from the Covid-19 pandemic. It was noted that Claimants' Counsel did not suggest that the duty was as wide as that. But submitted that the duty was owed to residents of care homes for the elderly (such as the deceased) because of their exceptional vulnerability to fatal infection by Covid-19.

The Court then examined medical treatment cases as it considered that they provided some guidance.

It referenced *Lopes de Sousa Fernandez v Portugal* (2017) 66 EHRR 28 concerning a denial of access to medical treatment. The court held that in cases involving alleged medical negligence the State's positive obligations were regulatory, including *'necessary measures to ensure implementation, including supervision and enforcement'*. It noted that medical negligence cases in which States had been held liable under

Article 2 are '*exceptional ones in which the fault attributable to the health care providers went beyond a mere error or medical negligence..*'. The court went on to say that a deficiency in the regulatory framework is not in itself sufficient to raise an issue under Article 2. The State's obligation to regulate must be understood in a broader sense. It is only in 'very exceptional circumstances' that Article 2 may be engaged. Two types of exceptional circumstances were provided. Firstly a situation where a patient's life is knowingly put in danger by denial of access to life-saving emergency treatment; and secondly where a systemic or structural dysfunction in hospital services results in a patient being deprived of access to life-saving emergency treatment and the authorities knew or ought to have known about that risk and failed to undertake the necessary measures to prevent that risk from materialising, thus putting the patients' lives in danger.

Consideration was given to the well-known case of *Watts v United Kingdom* (2020) 51 EHRR SE5. This concerned the Council's intention to move a 106 year old resident of a care home that intended to be closed down because it did not meet the physical space standards imposed by legislation. It was held that the State did owe an Article 2 duty to the applicant but her claim failed as being declared inadmissible. Having regard to the operational choices in the provision of residential care to the elderly and the careful planning and steps which were undertaken to minimise any risk to the applicant's life, the Court considered that the authorities had met their positive obligations under Article 2.

This is a useful case for recalling that article 2 imposes both negative and positive obligations on the State. The negative obligation prohibits the intentional and unlawful taking of life by agents of the state. The positive obligation ...requires that they take appropriate steps to safeguard lives. This implies a positive obligation to take preventive operational measures to protect an individual whose life is at risk.

Para 83 of *Watts*: '*For the court to find a violation of the positive obligation to protect life, it must be established that the authorities knew or ought to have known at the time of a real and immediate risk to the life of an identified individual and that they failed to take measures which, judged reasonably might have been expected to avoid that risk. The court reiterates that the scope of any positive obligation must be interpreted in a way which does not impose an impossible or disproportionate burden on the authorities, including in respect of the operational choices which must be made in terms of authorities and resources. Accordingly, not every claimed risk to life can entail for the authorities a Convention requirement to take operational measures to prevent that risk from materialising'.*

The Court referenced Baroness Hale who remarked in her judgment of *Rabone* whilst commenting on the above passage, that such broad statements of principle are hard to interpret and even harder to apply. She went on to say that it could be tempting, as per the neighbour principle in *Donoghue v Stevenson* [1932] AC 562, to treat it as the statement of duty explained in para 82 of *Watts* and is breached in the circumstances set out in para 83. She questioned whether in fact the *Watts* decision was laying down a broad principle that the State had a duty, if the authorities know or ought to know of a real and immediate risk to the life of an individual, to take such measures as might reasonably be expected of them to avoid that risk. In the case of *Watts* the extent of the duty depended upon the extent of the risk, on which the evidence was equivocal.

The court having reviewed the environmental and medical cases, distilled some principles from the domestic and Strasbourg cases:

i. A real and immediate risk to life is a necessary but not sufficient factor for the existence of an Article 2 operational duty;

ii. The other necessary factor is the assumption by the State of responsibility for the welfare and safety of particular individuals, of whom prisoners, detainees under mental health legislation, immigration detainees and conscripts are paradigm examples since they are under State control;

iii. However, the duty may exist even in the absence of an assumption by the State of responsibility, where the State or municipal authorities have become aware of dangerous situations involving a specific threat to life which arise exceptionally from risks posed by the violent and unlawful acts of others *(Osman)* or man-made hazards *(Oneryildiz, Kolyadenko)* or natural hazards *(Budayeva),* or from appalling conditions in residential care facilities of which the authorities had become aware *(Nencheva, Campeanu);*

iv. *Watts* suggests that, in exceptional circumstances (which remain so far undefined), the operational duty may also arise where State or municipal authorities engage in activities which they know or should know pose a real and immediate risk (according to *Maguire,* an exceptional risk) to the life of a vulnerable individual or group of individuals.

The court reminded itself of Lord Bingham's statement in *R (Ullah) v Special Adjudicator* [2004] UKHL 26 that Parliament never intended by enacting the Human Rights Act 1998 to give UK courts the power to give a more generous scope to the Convention rights than that which was to be found in the jurisprudence of the Strasbourg court.

With that in mind no doubt, the Court noted that there was no authority in Strasbourg as holding the State under an operational duty to take al reasonable steps to avoid the real and immediate risk to life posed by an epidemic or pandemic to as broad and undefined a sector of the population as residents of care homes for the elderly. No such duty exists. They recognised that (the UK courts) should keep pace with the Strasbourg jurisprudence, but not run past it and disappear into the distance.

As a consequence the Court found that the Defendants did not owe the Article 2 operational duty.

Issues surrounding the 'disproportionate burden' and 'margin' as well as causation did not arise.

Article 8

This is the right to respect for private and family life, his home and correspondence.

This was relied upon by the Claimants citing *Stoicescu v Romania* [2011] ECHR 1193 (26 July 2011) which concerned a woman who had been attacked by stray dogs in Bucharest and suffered debilitating health conditions. The ECHR held that Romania had violated article 8 of the Convention through failing to take sufficient measures to protect the physical and psychological integrity of the applicant. Such injury, the Court held amounted to 'private life'. The authorities had broad and detailed information on the threat posed by stray dogs in Bucharest but did nothing to combat it. The Claimants argued that *Stoicescu* was important because it added a broader approach to engagement of duty, demonstrating a positive obligation owed to the entirety of the Bucharest population to protect them from the known risk of stray dogs.

The Claimant's senior Counsel argued that Article 8 was relevant as it met the Defendants' threshold objections to Article 2; that it protected the right for home where many people had become sick and died; and that Article 8 was the Convention right that would cover the provision of information to the public regarding a threat to life.

It was submitted by the Claimants (citing *Vilnes v Norway* 5 December 2013, unreported), that a claim under Article 8 may succeed where Article 2 fails. But the Court demurred, stating that the present case was not about the provision of information to care home residents about the risk to their lives from the pandemic, but about the substance of policy decisions and the documents embodying them.

The Article 8 claim therefore failed.

The judicial review claim

This is a claim under the common law but for ease of classification, the author has kept this separate from the Equality Act claims. The court examined whether the decisions and policies made were unlawful by the standards of public law. They examined the facts as presented to the Defendants at the relevant time, and not applying the benefit of hindsight. The test was whether the decisions taken fell outside the range of reasonable decisions properly open to the Government in the light of the knowledge then available and the circumstances then existing.

The court also recognised that scientific knowledge was uncertain and rapidly changing in respect of a novel disease. The circumstances were pressurised where the matters at stake were of the utmost gravity. There were practical limitations such as the worldwide shortage of PPE.

Risk of transmission

This concerned the Claimants' criticism of the perceived risk of community transmission. They referred to the document entitled *'Guidance for social or community care and residential settings on COVID-19'* dated 25 February 2020. It contained the statement that there was currently no community transmission of COVID-19 and that it was therefore *'very unlikely that anyone receiving care in a care home or the community will become infected'.* Yet on 5 March 2020, according to Claimants' Counsel, there was sustained community transmission in the UK, noted by SAGE.

The Court did not find any unlawfulness in the 25 February document; the outbreak of the virus in the UK was at a very early stage and it was not until 28 February that the `UK reported its first COVID-19 case with no link to travel abroad.

Scientific evidence

The High Court referred to the developing nature of the scientific evidence, holding that while it was undoubtedly right that there was no scientific proof in mid-March 2020 that asymptomatic transmission was occurring, it was well recognised by the experts that such transmission was *possible.*

The Court stated:

> *'...the fact that evidence is not conclusive does not mean that it carries no weight. Ministers were obliged to weigh up not just the likelihood that non-symptomatic transmission was occurring, but also the very serious consequences if it did so. Non-symptomatic transmission would mean that one elderly patient moved from hospital to a care home could infect other residents before manifesting symptoms or even without ever manifesting symptoms. In this context it is important to recall the emphasis laid by the Defendants on the fact that they were intending to adopt the precautionary principle, in essence preparing on the basis that the worst could happen, throughout their response to COVID-19.*

At para 278, the Court found that '*the growing appreciation that asymptomatic transmission was a real possibility ought to have prompted a change in Government policy concerning care homes earlier than it did*'.

The Court then examined and ruled on the 4 policies set out earlier.

In essence they did not criticise the **first policy** – the 'March PHE Policy' concerning advice about visitors to care homes It was unrealistic for the Claimants to say on 13 March a ban on all visiting was the only rational course for the Defendants to have pursued. The Court justified this conclusion based on the 'very early stage' of the outbreak and the fact that whilst 'there was some evidence in the literature that people could become infected before developing symptoms...there was little evidence of transmission from asymptomatic cases'.

As a result the guidance about visits was not irrational, nor did it fail to take into account relevant considerations given the state of scientific knowledge at that stage.

The **second policy**

The Court rejected as 'unrealistic' the sustained attack on the Hospital Discharge Policy. It was appraised of the concerns raised by the Claimants that the NHS might be overwhelmed by the increasing numbers of seriously ill patients. The fact that its expanded capacity was never breached did not assist the Claimants' argument. The NHS was using temporary overflow facilities at venues such as the ExCel conference centre. There was nothing unlawful in the discharge policy contained within documents of 17-19 March 2020.

The Court also did not accept the Claimants' suggestion that discharge from hospital to care home should have been subject to an assessment of each care home to provide safe care.

The Court was also against the suggestion that the Government should have made provision for testing in March; there were simply not enough test kits. The Defendants could not be said to have acted irrationally by agreeing a prioritisation list.

The **third policy**

The *Admissions Guidance* published 2 April 2020 stated that patients who may have COVID-19, whether symptomatic or not could be safely cared for in a care home if this guidance is followed. The Court found there was no evidence that the Secretary of State or anyone advising him addressed the issue of the risk to care home residents of asymptomatic transmission.

The Court also held that there was a failure to take into account the risk of asymptomatic transmission to elderly and vulnerable residents. It was not until 15 April in the Action Plan that testing and isolation for 14 days was recommended for new residents admitted to care homes. The Court stated:

> *'This was a significant delay at a critical period. We consider that the decision to issue the 2 April Admissions Guidance in that form was irrational in that it failed to take into account the risk of asymptomatic transmission, and failed to make an assessment of the balance of risks.'*

The **fourth policy**

The Court considered it unrealistic that the 15 April Action Plan did not address the risk of transmission of the disease to residents from staff. They also did not accept as a ground for JR the wording '*may wish*' to isolate new residents.

This concerns the lawfulness of a decision or action by a public body that is examined by the court. It is not the conclusion that is significant but rather the method in which the decision was made.

<u>Summary of the judgment</u>

There was a partial finding of unlawfulness of guidance documents issued during the course of the pandemic. The March Discharge Policy and the April Admissions Guidance failed to take into account the risk to elderly and vulnerable residents of asymptomatic transmission. The Government had failed to adequately plan for the best way to manage those who had been discharged. There should have been a change in Government policy earlier than it did. Discharged patients should have been isolated until all risk of transmission of infection had passed. So the policy set out in each document was irrational in failing to advise that where an asymptomatic patient was admitted to a care home, they should have been kept apart from other residents for 14 days.

So the public law claim succeeded in part against the First and Third Defendants. It failed completely against the Second Defendant.

The Court was sympathetic to the difficulties facing government decision makers seeking to evaluate novel scientific knowledge in very pressurised circumstances.

3.2 RAMIFICATIONS OF GARDNER

It has been established that The Government through the Secretary of State was held not liable in public law about its advice concerning care home visitors because they did not have the legal power to require care homes to admit patients. But what about potential liabilities of the 97% care homes in the private sector or third sector?

It is conceivable that claims brought in negligence against care homes could 'pray in aid' the failure of care home owners and their managers through vicarious liability for not shutting down the homes to visitors who carried the risk of transmitting the virus. It is known that knowledge about asymptomatic transmission changed over the course of time. As the judges found in *Gardner* at para 278, there should have been a change in Government policy when asymptomatic transmission became a real possibility.

One might say that such a claim may face considerable difficulties when private individuals and corporations would be deemed liable to act against national policy. Defendants would not be judged with the benefit of hindsight.[31]

Amnesty International had found that some care homes decided at an early stage of the pandemic *not* to follow the guidance because of developments in the transfer of the virus in Spain and Italy.

The tenor of the judgment in *Gardner* was to sympathise with government decision makers in very difficult times and where scientific knowledge was unfolding. Nevertheless there was some limited victory for the Claimants.

As the Court was keen to point out that there has been no successful ECHR care regarding medical treatment in care homes. And those claims failed here too. The wider public law challenges to key decisions and policies were also rejected.

Where they came unstuck were the March and April 2020 policies about the risk to elderly and vulnerable residents from asymptomatic transmission. There should have been advice that new entrants to care homes should, so far as practicable, be kept isolated from other residents for 14 days. The Government has not appealed this decision and perhaps wisely considered that the limited findings against them with regards to policies in force for a relatively short period may not be sufficient to open the floodgates in damages claims.

There were two interlocutory hearings concerning applications for specific disclosure and the use of expert evidence. On appeal, these applications were refused. The Defendants did provide general disclosure that was widespread, though the Claimants sought specific disclosure of ministerial submissions to the Secretary of State about the four policies. The Claimants were not satisfied about disclosure and

31 Roe v Minister of Health and Another (1954) 2 WLR 1 (QB). The Court assesses reasonableness in the particular circumstances and would reflect the emergency situation when assessing breach.

subsequent comment by the Claimants' solicitor post judgment reflected some criticism of trying complex matters in the administrative court. Presumably this was based on the comments made by the 1st instance judge that the court was not facing the same hard-edged factual questions than in the case relied upon as authority. Clearly they were concerned about the duty of candour or rather the lack of it.

The duty of candour is enshrined in NHS bodies as a statutory requirement under the *Health and Social Care Act 2008.* Healthcare professionals also have an ethical duty of candour. This underlines the need to be open and honest with patients. But does it extend to disclosure of minutes of meetings between health professionals during the course of a patients' treatment. This might relate to an adverse incident, for example. You would hope so but it may not form part of standard disclosure. In *Gardner* the Claimants only sought declarations and therefore one might say that in the light of information overload and a hard-pressed court that some disclosure that might have been beneficial to Claimants was withheld.

It is suggested that the test for specific disclosure in a clinical negligence claim under **Part 31.12** and **PD 31A** of the **Civil Procedure Rules** – requiring as it does the court's application of the overriding objective – would have been more likely to result in granting the application.

In any private civil claim, disclosure and expert evidence would be permitted, though it is anticipated that that would relate to claims against care homes and/or NHS Trusts rather than government departments. Although expert witnesses did not feature in the *Gardner* case, there is public record of experts advising the government and extracts are referred to in the case. To what extent a civil judge applies weight to their pronouncements is open to question but the author suggests it may be minimal.

There may well be benefits in quoting from some of the findings given by experts and from expert committees in the *Gardner judgment.* By way of example, the Defendants received advice from the Chief Medical officer and the `Chief Scientific Officer, as well as from specialist expert committees, SAGE, NERVTAG, SPI-M and the UKSCG. The experts appeared to accept that more information was required from January 2020. In particular Professor Gordon, Professor of Care of Older People at the University of Nottingham at para 64 quoted a published study of 8 march 2020 relating to pre-symptomatic transmission for Singapore and China. This suggested that pre-symptomatic transmission of COVID-19 constituted a very substantial proportion of all transmission.

On 9th March, the Health Minister, Lord Bethell referred to in the judgment at par 65 said in the House of Lords that '*large numbers of people are infectious or infected but are completely asymptomatic and never go near a test kit*'.

The legal test in this JR case is different from that which a Claimant must satisfy in a clinical negligence claim. In the former it is a reasonableness test; the Court must ask whether the decisions taken fell outside the range of reasonable decisions properly open to the Government in the light of the knowledge then available and the circumstances then existing. Causation still featured but was accepted in *Gardner*. Clinical negligence requires an objective assessment by reference to the *Bolam* duty, namely acting in accordance with a responsible body of medical opinion, provided that such opinion is logical. It will require the Claimant to obtain expert evidence on breach of duty and causation.

It is significant that *Gardner* decided that there was **enough** scientific evidence in March and April 2020 for reasonable suspicion that a person could show no symptoms from the virus but still be able to affect others. The court held that the Secretary of State for Health and Social Care should have been cautious and ordered a two-week period of self-isolation for every discharged patient at that time. The junior Minister, Rt Hon. Helen Whateley did raise serious concerns about the risk of asymptomatic spread but appeared to have been overruled.

The most salient and first question that will arise in a private clinical negligence claim is who should be the Defendant? Usual considerations are the owner of the care home, possibly the managing agent if they assume responsibility. There are arguments that care homes with the benefit of medical personnel, should have been on notice about the risks of Covid transmission. Dependant on the time frame as to when information became available, they could be deemed to know (or should have known) about the risks of asymptomatic transmission; and that allowing visitors or even new patients from hospitals could place existing (vulnerable) residents at risk of infection and really serious illness. Should they have taken it upon themselves to require isolation of new patients in the form of quarantine or simply refused new residents.

An argument would surely be presented that care homes should have had their own form of lockdown (before that instituted by Government). Although care homes were not required to receive hospital patients, there was pressure to do so by Government. In following Government guidance (or rather the lack of guidance about asymptomatic isolation), should a care home provider escape liability?

Gardner provides some limited assistance it is suggested, in that Claimants may consider it prudent (subject to reflecting on costs implications and appropriate after the event insurance cover), to widen the pool of potential Defendants to include possibly the Secretary of State for Health and Social Care.

Causation will be difficult to establish from whom a resident was infected with Covid-19 where visitors were permitted to attend and where staff did not live on the premises. Much investigation would need to examine staff rotas and Covid tests. Issues of medical confidentiality and data protection would require staff to voluntarily disclose their medical records. Much would depend on the individual care home's policy towards testing and level of comprehensiveness. A national testing programme was not announced by the Secretary of State for Health until the 2nd April 2020. Public Health England commenced a surveillance study on the 3rd April. On 15th April, the government published its social care action plan requiring that all patients discharged from hospital be tested for Covid-19.

It will be fact specific of staff movements and those of visitors and the policies employed by the individual care homes. Future Claimants seeking to rely upon *Gardner* do face significant hurdles to overcome, including:

- If private care homes had received the appropriate advice to isolate residents as far as reasonably practicable from 19 March 2020, what would they have done?

- And if they had done something differently, what would the outcome have been in relation to Covid-19 infections, deaths and serious illnesses. Will the Courts accept an increased material contribution argument.

In December 2022, it was reported that Letters of Claim had been sent by a firm of Solicitors representing families of deceased relatives who had died in care homes after contracting Covid-19 in the early stages of the pandemic in 2020. The claims were brought in the light of the *Gardner* judgment. They reminded the Health Secretary and Health Security Agency that the policies were irrational in failing to advise that where an asymptomatic patient was admitted to a care home, they should be kept apart from other residents for 14 days and there were many deaths as a result of the failure to take account of the growing appreciation that asymptomatic transmission was a real possibility.

In the light of (presumed) denials of liability and the failure of some Defendants to extend the Limitation period, proceedings were issued in the High Court in August 2023 seeking damages for loss of life, personal injuries, pain and suffering, anxiety and distress and feelings of justice. The Defendants were individual care homes, Hospital Trusts and the Secretary of State for Health and Social Care. The claims were brought alleging a breach of Articles 2,8 and 14 of the ECHR and section 6 of the HRA 1998 that relates to the acts of Public Bodies.

The families say that breach of human rights occurred by the State's failure to (i) protect the right to life (ii) respect the right to private and family life (iii) protect the right not to be discriminated against.

The Claimants will be inviting the Court to determine whether the decisions taken in the early weeks of the pandemic were reasonable; if not did those decisions cause or contribute to loss of life. The current state of the proceedings is not known publically. Given the multiple Defendants, it is conceivable that some may result in settlement on without prejudice terms and subject to a confidentiality clause. We may really only know the outcome should the claims go to trial.

3.3 OTHER CASES

There have not been that many reported claims against care homes involving the HRA so the impact of *Gardner* has been muted. Probably this reflects the difficulties in meeting the minimum threshold of *'real and immediate risk to life'*. This was tested in the case of *Milner v Barchester Healthcare Homes Ltd*[32]. An elderly woman with dementia died from pneumonia after being subject to neglect (as found by the CQC). A friend of the deceased pursued a claim against the care home and Local Authority seeking damages for alleged breaches of Article 2 and 3 of the ECHR in the provision of care. The Defendants challenged the status of the Claimant as an indirect victim, as not having standing, and argued that the Articles were not engaged as the thresholds for meeting the tests were not met. The Claimant discontinued against the Local Authority and the case against the care home was first heard at a summary judgment hearing where the care home sought dismissal of the proceedings. It was held that Article 2 was

---

32 [2022] EWHC 593(QB)

not satisfied because the high threshold of a *'real and immediate risk to life'* was not met. There was no evidence to link the cause of death to choking. Article 2 also failed on causation with respect to a *'systems failure'* to maintain and implement appropriate administrative measures and safeguards to protect the lives of residents as that had not caused her death. The claim regarding Article 3 would go to trial to ascertain the severity of treatment. Such factors would include: duration of treatment, physical and mental effects and state of health to ascertain whether they met the threshold of '*degrading and inhuman treatment*'.

The outcome of the trial (assuming it went to trial) is not known as not being reported. Most cases will be relatives and therefore direct victims so the issue of 'standing' is unlikely to arise. Claimants will need to give careful consideration as to whether an HRA claim is viable in meeting high threshold criteria rather than simply piggy backing clinical negligence claims.

It seems that there are more reported cases on Covid at Inquest hearings – perhaps not that surprising. A case of some importance is *Gareth Roberts and Domingo David*, heard before the Senior Coroner for South Wales Central. These two nurses died from Covid-19 in March/April 2020 whilst working at hospitals under the Cardiff and Vale University Health Board. Mr Roberts was vulnerable having Type 2 diabetes. Was he provided with appropriate PPE at the hospital? The inquest explored national guidance in terms of infection prevention and control, cohorting of Covid-19 patients, PPE and risk assessment of employees. Other employees developed Covid symptoms or tested positive such that the Coroner (after hearing from medical expert witnesses and Public Health Wales) concluded that both Mr Roberts and Ms David contracted Covid at work. He went further and held that the deaths were from industrial disease.

This case has important implications for inquests and families seeking an industrial disease verdict. Firstly it may persuade a Coroner to hold an inquest when there is doubt about human error or not. It probably has broader appeal to workplace settings beyond the health and social care sectors where an inquest is more likely indicated than where the Coroner is focussed on whether a death was otherwise potentially unnatural. If caused by industrial disease it is 'unnatural'. Secondly such a verdict would clearly assist in a future civil claim and go some way to proving causation. After all, the inquest may be treated as a 'dry test run' in hearing experts opine on causation. It would be a bold court that would reject outright an inquest's findings. Thirdly, although not authoritative, the court refused to engage Article 2 HRA.

An inquest case of *Leilani Medel* was a health worker at a care home in South Wales where evidence was brought of a shortage of PPE. She contracted Covid-19 at the care home and died from it. The Coroner held that Mrs Medel was likely to have come into contact with the virus when other patients exhaled particles. He gave a narrative verdict that she 'contracted Covid-19 whilst working at the Anwen care home'. However he was not persuaded to find that Covid was an industrial disease.

In the Inquest of *Matthew Dale* heard at the Cheshire coroner's court in January 2023, the Coroner found that he died of misadventure, contributed by a missed opportunity to identify his needs. Mr Dale died after choking on an incontinence pad while resident in a care home. He lacked capacity to make decisions for himself. It was argued on behalf of the family that the failures in his care amounted to neglect and a breach of Article 2 ECHR on both operational and systemic grounds. Such failures amounted to negligence, firstly in the absence of any system to prevent his access to the pad, and secondly the fact that he was left alone unsupervised. The human rights claim failed with the Coroner finding that there was a 'breakdown in communication' between the commissioners and the care home that did not amount to a systematic failure. There were also no operational failures that presented a 'real and immediate' risk as there had been no clinical presentation of him putting non-food items into his mouth. Further, there was no neglect as he had not suffered a 'total and complete' lack of care.

The case of *Maguire, R (on the application of) v His Majesty's Senior Coroner for Blackpool & Fylde and Anor*[33] explores Article 2 Right to life. The case went to the Supreme Court (SC) on appeal from the Court of Appeal that heard the appeal of an Inquest into the death of Ms Maguire. She died in hospital from pneumonia and peritonitis. She had been in a care home and initially refused to go to hospital. The Coroner had refused to give an expanded verdict as to how the deceased came by her death and instead directed the jury to give a standard verdict. The SC examined whether there was a systems duty on the part of the care home to trigger an enhanced procedural obligation. The Coroner at first instance examined the systems in place at the care home and concluded that there was no arguable breach. The SC upheld this, finding that there may have been individual lapses but the systems were such that a proper standard of care was provided to residents. They equally dismissed the allegation of breach of the systems duty on the part of healthcare providers. The SC also dismissed the appeal of an operational duty on the part of the care home, finding that the care home did look after the deceased and permitted her access to healthcare available to the population at large. They further dismissed the allegation of breach of the operational duty against other healthcare providers, holding that the deceased should enjoy personal autonomy and that the clinicians were not on notice that her life was in danger.

A completely different case not concerning a care home but the principles from *Harris v Bartrums Haulage and Storage Ltd and another*[34] will apply in employers' liability claims. It is not treading new ground in emphasising the importance of training and risk assessments necessary to discharge the duty of care. This has striking relevance when reviewing what workplace precautions were instituted during the pandemic to reduce the risk of Covid infections. The Claimant was driving a tractor and got out to couple a trailer. He did not put on the handbrake such that the tractor rolled away striking him and causing

33 UKSC 20 (21 June 2023)

34 [2020] EWHC 900 (QB)

injuries. Although he was given a handbook to read that explained his job role, he did not read it. The judge found that the employer had breached its duty of care in relation to training and risk assessments. The judge was mindful of the employer's common law duty of care representing the '*reasonable and prudent employer, taking positive thought for the safety of his workers in light of what he knows or ought to know..*'.[35] The judge nevertheless dismissed the claim on causation and would have made a finding of 80% contributory negligence.

The significance of this case underlines the importance of the 'six-pack' regulations as being significant in proving breach of duty under the common law. In Covid times, an employers' liability claim will focus on training and compliance with government and HSE guidance on hygiene standards, social distancing, PPE etc.

There have been reports of a group of doctors – 'Long Covid Doctors for Action' launching a class action for personal injuries sustained in the course of their employment after contracting Covid and failing to recover. Solicitors were instructed, though the outcome is not known. It would be expected that the potential Defendants would be NHS Trusts, GP Practices (indemnified by The Clinical Negligence Scheme for General Practice) and The Secretary of State for Health and Social Care. One should not forget that healthcare workers worked in the frontline and exposed themselves to considerable risk. Their statutory employment rights to ensure a safe system and place of work were no less diminished than others. Claims may have been commenced, and possibly still could be pursued, (subject to limitation and date of knowledge arguments) by those clinicians who were employed in care or nursing homes or provided domiciliary services.

---

35 Quotation taken from Stokes v Guest [1968] 1 WLR 1776

CHAPTER FOUR

DEFENDANTS

4.1 CARE HOMES

Who to sue? There must be owed a duty of care in establishing negligence. The starting point will be the owners or operators of the Care Home where someone has contracted Covid-19 in the home. This is likely to be owned by a corporate organisation so a Companies House search[36] will be required to confirm ownership. It will be the name of the company rather than its trading name that will be the appropriate Defendant. Where the home is owned by an individual or partners then the convention is to name in the Particulars of Claim the individuals as first, second defendant etc. and their trading name. The *Business Names Act* 1985 requires that sole traders, partners or a company specify on their letterhead the name and address of the owner or Director. If more than 20 partners their names may be inspected (if not displayed) at the business address.

In all likelihood confirmation of the correct business entity will be established through exchange of correspondence – and certainly by the receipt of the letter of Response – from the insurers representing the proposed Defendant.

Much depends on the cause of action that will be brought. For claims against Care homes, negligence and breach of statutory duty would be expected to be the usual allegations. The principles of vicarious liability are such that an employer is responsible for the negligent acts or omissions of an employee. This would apply where an allegation concerned a Covid infection received from a member of staff. Where a

---

36 find-and-update.company-information.service.gov.uk

visitor introduced the infection then the home is still likely to be liable for failing to introduce sufficient safety precautions in screening visitors or refusing access.

Useful information may be gleaned from inspection reports undertaken by the Care Quality Commission (CQC). Since 2018 they have been designated as the lead enforcement regulator of safety and quality of treatment and care. Part of their remit is to assess and manage the risk of infection.

The starting point is determining where the infection occurred. For most Claimants, it will be in their home in a care home. From whom was the infection contracted? More difficult to determine of course, unless the number of people coming into contact with the Claimant was strictly limited and where there has been regular testing. It may be a process of elimination. But does a Claimant need to establish the identity of the person who infected them to establish the Defendant. Not necessarily so long as they may establish how they were infected. If they have not had any outside visitors so community infection is excluded, inferences could be made that it occurred in the care home. One would need to examine procedures on visitor access, shielding and social distancing, regular testing, hygiene practices, training and appropriate and effective use of PPE as examples. Here again inferences may be necessary as to when the Claimant may have been exposed and on balance due to insufficiently robust safeguards.

4.2 LOCAL AUTHORITIES

Many residents of Care Homes live there full-time because of physical or mental health constraints. They (or family members) will have arranged their own accommodation. Some may stay for respite care and therefore remain part-time. Others may have their care and support arranged by their Local Authority by virtue of s.18 *Care Act 2014.* The Local Authority must assess the person's care and support needs and then consider how those needs will be met, whether it be in a Care home, their own home or via community provision. Section 19 of the Act provides that accommodation is made available to a person with no recourse to public funds and where care and support does not meet the eligibility threshold but nevertheless could give rise to a breach of human rights. An assessment is made under s.9 of the Act.

Whilst a Local Authority must be mindful of human rights' issues, it will also have raised a duty of care by complying with its statutory responsibilities. And those duties in the time of Covid were significant. Because it could be argued that by placing a resident in a Care home that did not have sufficient safeguards in place, renders the Authority potentially liable in negligence should a resident have contracted Covid or developed complications arising from the infection. Section 9(4) of the Care Act specifies that the needs assessment must identify a person's care and support needs and its impact on all aspects of wellbeing. At its heart the Act requires under section 42 for Local Authorities to ensure there is safeguarding oversight from abuse or neglect.

Though the responsibilities under the Care Act were tempered by the *Coronavirus Act 2020* which introduced Care Act 'easements' from 31 March 2020. This permitted Local Authorities to reduce their usual duties such as completing detailed assessments of people's care and support needs, or to carry out financial assessments. They did not have to prepare or review care and support plans although person-centred care planning was still required. Essentially authorities were given the power to prioritise. That said, the guidance made clear that Local Authorities remained under a duty to meet needs where otherwise it would breach an individual's human rights under the ECHR. The relevant articles are the right to life under Article 2, the right to freedom from inhuman and degrading treatment under Article 3 and the right to private and family life under Article 8. Safeguarding duties still remained paramount and Local Authorities' duties relating to prevention and providing information and advice also remained in place.

So it can be argued that the principal statutory responsibilities to ensure wellbeing and advice remain at the core of the authorities' functions; and any derogation that exposes a resident to Covid in circumstances that were foreseeable – or where there may have been a failure to vet a Care home's safety would expose an Authority to a liability potentially in negligence, breach of human rights and breach of its statutory duties.

4.3 HOSPITAL NHS TRUSTS

For NHS treatment in a hospital, it will be the NHS Trust that is a potential Defendant. Treatment in a private hospital for a private patient may render the hospital owner or operator potentially liable, but it could be the treating doctor (or other clinician) who has personal liability. They may operate a contract for service with the hospital and thereby be an independent contractor. As such they are not employed by the hospital and offer their services by arrangement. They would have to take out their own Medical Defence indemnity insurance. Most frequently when a patient undergoes a procedure, their agreement is with the private hospital provider. Therefore when considering who is the likely Defendant, care must be taken to establish the precise contractual arrangements. There is a strong likelihood that the potential Defendant will still be the private hospital and in litigation they may seek an indemnity or contribution from the contracting doctor or surgeon and join them into the proceedings. Clarity should be established before proceedings are issued.

Those Claimants receiving private treatment have potential claims in contract and tort (negligence). However, general damages would not be duplicated if both causes of action were brought. Conceivably part reimbursement of fees payable for treatment may be recoverable in a breach of contract claim for lack of consideration.

Some NHS patients receive their care in a private hospital because of availability and resources. They still remain NHS patients and the NHS still exercises its duty of care and therefore retains liability.

Where the allegation concerns transfer of a hospital patient into a care home without testing them so constituting omissions of care then the Defendant may be the NHS Trust providing treatment. The dilemma will be whether two defendants are sued for potential negligence. In the example given, liability may well attach to both the care home and NHS Trust. Careful consideration must be given in relation to costs and the possibility of incurring wasted costs in the event that liability attaches to only one Defendant. The issue may be whether each Defendant is liable for separate breaches of duty or whether the acts or omissions are caused by the Defendants acting in concert, or by concurrence. If the damage is contraction of Covid, the allegations against separate Defendants will be different, though there may be overlapping claims. Ultimately only one Defendant may be liable; but it may not be possible to determine from which location exposure occurred. One could foresee a care home arguing that it relied on information and guidance provided by another party – the NHS Trust or the Health Secretary, perhaps. The NHS Trust might argue that potential breach in the safeguarding duties imposed at a Care home constituted a new or intervening act, absolving them of liability. The temptation for a Claimant anticipating these arguments may be to pursue several Defendants, at least in the early stages to tease out their response and obtain early disclosure.

4.4 SECRETARY OF STATE FOR HEALTH AND SOCIAL CARE

This is the government department run by the Health Secretary responsible for management of the NHS and Social Care. We use terminology to describe the government, Secretary of State, Health Secretary and Department of Health interchangeably but they represent the same Defendant, namely the Secretary of State for Health and Social Care.

Whilst not directly or personally responsible to fulfil the statutory duties set out in the *National Health Service Act 2006*, they are accountable for the decisions taken on behalf of the government. Duties are in practice delegated to Strategic Health Authorities and Primary Care Trusts under section 7 of the Act. The Secretary of State sets objectives and standing rules for clinical commissioning groups and the NHS Commissioning Board. In essence the role is one of policy making and oversight.

The Secretary of State is legally liable for the provision of services in accordance with his duty under section 1(2) of the Act (through delegation effectively) and may be subject to judicial review by a member of the public. In fact this did indeed happen in the *Gardner* judgment discussed in chapter 3. Policies and the decisions issued by the government during the pandemic were subject to scrutiny in their capacity as a public body. The documents deemed unlawful were dated 17 and 19 March 2020 and 2 April 2020 because they failed to take into account the risk to elderly and vulnerable residents from non-asymptomatic transmission of Covid. It was not until mid-April 2020 that the Secretary of State advised that asymptomatic patients admitted to a care home should isolate for 14 days. That omission to advise was held to be irrational. The court found a lack of evidence that the government had considered whether the policies should have advised of this risk. The government had suggested that it had relied upon evidence from Public Health England in framing its policies. But that did not impress the court given that the government's own public health advisor, Sir Patrick Vallance had stated the potential risk for asymptomatic transmission as early as 13 March 2020.

The Court was not prepared to give the benefit of the doubt to the Defendant on its decision- making in the absence of supporting documentary evidence. This was notwithstanding the inevitable pressure under which the government was operating. It underlines the need that a paper trail and cogent statements are important in judicial review as in other litigation claims.

A government department is not going to be the first Defendant that a Claimant will consider pursuing unless the claim is for judicial review or perhaps under the HRA. As mentioned in chapter 5, judicial review is not without its difficulties for a private individual seeking recompense for sustaining injury. However, there is scope for care homes to rely upon guidance and policies issued by the government in their defence of a claim under the common law. Where such guidance was wrong and held to be irrational and unlawful, one may consider that a possible Defendant in negligence could well be the Secretary of State for Health and Social Care. This may arise where a care home might bring contribution proceedings under Part 20 CPR to join in the Department of Health. Or the Claimant may decide following receipt of a Defence to apply to bring in the government as a further Defendant. As touched on earlier, there could well be a backlog of cases that may have been stayed, pending the outcome of the Public Inquiry. If there are more revelations that may assist Claimants, it may be that, provided limitation is protected, further evidence will determine the direction of the claim and the number of Defendants.

The Secretary of State is currently subject to litigation for breach of Articles 2,8 and 14 ECHR by Claimants acting on behalf of the estate of deceased care home residents and a hospital patient. The grounds are said to be a failure by the state in the early stages of the pandemic to protect the rights of families through failures to publish procedures, appropriate guidance, policies and/or rules that would allow the owners of residential care and nursing homes to implement.

Should the Claimants prevail, one outcome could see care home operators defending claims thus putting the government squarely in the sights of future Claimants.

4.5 SUING THE WRONG DEFENDANT

The temptation where there are potentially multiple Defendants – perhaps a Care home, a hospital, the government or a GP where all have been involved in someone's care, whether on a clinical or policy basis is to sue them all. That would become costly if proceedings are discontinued against some of them later down the track. Or errors may be down to a simple spelling mistake or using the incorrect title of a Defendant.

Multiple Defendants

Litigation must be conducted efficiently and proportionately[37] in applying the overriding objective of the Civil Procedure Rules (CPR). The claim will require careful investigation prior to dispatching the Letter of Claim and certainly before issuing proceedings. A Claimant will know the Defendant's arguments upon receipt of the Letter of Response. That will identify their correct title. But what if the case has developed and proceedings issued (perhaps for limitation purposes) against too many Defendants? A Claimant may discontinue all or part of a claim against one or more defendants[38] by serving a notice of discontinuance on all Defendants. By discontinuing, the Claimant is liable to pay wasted costs to the Defendant against whom the action is discontinued. The Claimant wherever possible should negotiate a discontinuance with that Defendant on the basis that there is no order as to costs prior to serving a notice of discontinuance. Of course the Defendant may not accept such terms and then it is down to reaching agreement on the best possible terms, perhaps by agreement to pay fixed costs and set out in a consent order.

[37] CPR 1.1(2) justly and proportionately

[38] CPR 38.2

Mistaken identity

Perhaps proceedings have been issued against a trading name rather than the corporate identity. Most likely the Claim Form and the Particulars of Claim wrongly detail the incorrect defendant.

This is covered under Part 17 of the CPR – Amendments to Statements of Case.

If the error is discovered before proceedings have been issued then an amendment is straightforward. The Defendant's name may be corrected or substituted with the correct Defendant at any time before service on the Defendant.

Once a claim is issued but before it is served, amendment is also straightforward as the Claimant may alter without consulting the other parties or the Court.

However, after proceedings have been issued and served on the Defendant, amendment requires the written consent of the Defendants or permission of the Court[39]. If permission is obtained only from the Defendant, it is conceivable that the Court may disallow amendments. It is advisable therefore to obtain permission from the Defendant, have it embodied in a Consent order and then filed with the Court to perfect the order.

Limitation

It becomes a little trickier once the primary limitation period has expired. Proceedings may have been issued in a rush to escape expiry of the limitation period and in haste an error has cropped up. Ideally this would not arise as the parties should have agreed a limitation extension in good time before expiry, or an automatic extension applies by virtue

[39] CPR 17.1(2)

of affiliation to the Covid-19 Clinical Negligence Protocol 2020 and its successor, the Clinical Negligence Claims Agreement 2024.

So amendment is governed by CPR 17.4 and will require approval by the Court. The Court may allow an amendment where it was a genuine mistake and the identity of the party was not in reasonable doubt. When the Court exercises its discretion, it always will have uppermost in its deliberations proportionality; that goes hand in glove with promptness and saving of costs.

By way of example, consider *Best Friends Group and another v Barclays Bank plc.*[40] The Claimant's solicitors issued proceedings using the Claimant's trading name (Best Friends Group) rather than the correct corporate entity (Best Friends Veterinary Group). Before service of proceedings, the Claim Form was amended but the Particulars of Claim was not. The documents were served. There was then some delay until the Claimant's solicitors applied to the Court for permission to add the owner as a Claimant but after expiry of the limitation period. At first instance the judge found insufficient evidence of a genuine mistake and that there could be reasonable doubt as to the identity of the Claimant. Were that not so, he was not persuaded to exercise his discretion because of unnecessary delay, costs and background to the error. The Court of Appeal agreed, dismissing the appeal as there is discretion in making case management decisions. Further there was no evidence by the Claimant himself about the application to amend the name and it was not made promptly.

So what is the morale to this story apart from the supercilious 'get it right the first time'. It can be difficult identifying the correct defendant when someone has received treatment from different healthcare providers. You may decide to send Letters of Claim to multiple Defendants and review their responses to ascertain whether they consider that they are appropriate Defendants. Expert evidence is

40 [2018] EWCA Civ 601

pivotal but at the pre-issue stage, this may be in short supply. At least screening reports should have been obtained disclosing potential claims. Have the correct specialists been approached? Where the principal treatment took place is a starting point. Given the title of this book, one would expect the focus to be on Care homes. Are they privately owned and what is their corporate status? If it is a Local authority care home then identify the correct name of the Authority (rather than the County Council).

CHAPTER FIVE

CAUSES OF ACTION

5.1 NEGLIGENCE

This is not intended to be a detailed exposition on the law of negligence in relation to clinical negligence claims but rather an overview as would apply to care homes.

Having said that, a brief resumé may be helpful in order to set the scene and assist with drafting the Letter of Claim and the Particulars of Claim.

Negligence in the clinical or medical context is the breach of duty to take care resulting in loss caused by that breach. So duty, breach, loss + causation = negligence. Those are the constituents in the mix for the Claimant to prove on the balance of probabilities.

For drafting purposes in setting out your allegations, 'breach' will equate to 'negligence', it being accepted that in most scenarios a care home will accept that it owes a duty of care.

Standard of care

The starting point remains the seminal case of *Bolam v Friern Hospital Management Committee* [1957] 1 WLR 582. The test is one of a responsible body of medical opinion, even if they be in the minority. It is a decision of fact to be determined by the judge in evaluating expert evidence as to whether treatment fell within acceptable practice.

The law therefore allows for different treatment options and different views.

Bolam was refined by *Bolitho v City and Hackney HA* [1996] 4 All ER 771 in that *'a responsible body'* must accord with a logical decision as determined by the court.

So applying the two tests a doctor (or another health professional) is not negligent if he or she acts in accordance with a responsible body of medical opinion, provided that the court finds such an opinion to be logical.

If representing a Claimant and the Defendant has expert evidence refuting the Claimant's on breach of duty, is it logical and sensible? An oft-quoted phrase from the court is this:

> *'..the court is not bound to hold that a defendant doctor escapes liability for negligent treatment or diagnosis just because he leads evidence from a number of medical experts...The court has to be satisfied that the exponents of the body of opinion relied upon can demonstrate that such opinion has a logical basis.'*

Therefore expert opinion is not necessarily the final arbiter as to whether a clinician has acted negligently. If the expert opinion appears illogical then the clinician could be deemed to have been negligent even if they have acted in accordance with it.

In many clinical negligence cases, causation is often the tricky element to prove and that won't be any less the case in some Covid claims where a resident has pre-existing conditions. A Defendant may accept some or all of the breaches but dispute causation. This is where expert evidence comes into play. Typically one may require an expert to address breach of duty and in all likelihood that would be a nurse practitioner with an elderly care physician opining on causation and injury. With causation of Covid or injuries resultant from that – or even loss of life emanating from that – then further expert evidence will be required (see Chapter 5).

There are two elements to causation:

(i) Legal causation is determined by the 'but for' test – but for the negligence, would the injury still have occurred. If there is more than one cause of the injury, then a modified test of material contribution applies. The negligence must have materially contributed to the damage/injury not just caused an increased risk of injury/loss. There must be no alternative complete cause of the injury. The material contribution test is only appropriate where there are multiple causes of the injury and only one cause cannot be established.

(ii) Factual causation is proving that the injury was caused by the defendant's failure.

According to an article by John de Bono KC[41], the consensus following the decision in *Bailey*[42] is that 'material contribution' is limited to cases where it is not possible to say what the outcome would have been absent the 'breach of duty'. Thus material contribution was applicable in indivisible injury cases.

There have been recent developments to refine the issue of causation even further since *Bailey*. The case of *Holmes v Poeton* [2023] EWCA Civ 1377 concerned the application of the material contribution test of causation to indivisible injury cases. This exemplified the problem where a disease is indivisible such as in Parkinson's disease, where the cause is not medically certain. There may be numerous causes that may contribute to the onset of the disease. So is the test for causation of damage by the Defendant's breach to be assessed by reference to the 'but for' or 'material contribution' test? Where an indivisible injury, causation can be established if the Defendant's breach was one of a

---

41 'Causation in Clinical Negligence Cases: Can there be liability where the same injury would probably have happened anyway?', 1st March 2024, John de Bono KC, UK Healthcare Law Blog

42 Bailey v Ministry of Defence [2009] 1 WLR 1052

number of causes of the injury and the defendant's breach materially contributed to the injury.

It is important to determine whether the Claimant suffers from a divisible or indivisible injury. If possible, a Claimant should try and prove that their injury is indivisible as recovery of damages will be more significant. Whole injury damages will be recoverable in full where the Claimant suffers from an indivisible injury. As compared to part damages where the Claimant suffers from a divisible injury that was materially contributed to by a defendant's breach. One has to determine the extent to which the defendant's breach materially contributed towards the injury to ascertain the portion of damage to which they contributed.

This begs the question as to whether the Covid infection is a discrete indivisible injury (we say it must be) and whether complications that may flow from that are divisible or indivisible. Here there may be less certainty and room for argument.

There is further complication as to which test the courts will apply to the Claimant's ultimate injuries or preceding injuries that lead to the ultimate injuries.

In order to cover both bases, it is suggested that the allegations plead that Covid and/or its complications were caused by the Defendant's breach of duty and in the alternative materially contributed to such injuries and loss. John de Bono KC suggests that the question to pose to experts is not only whether the breach of duty has 'materially contributed' to the outcome, but also whether it has contributed to the mechanism by which the injury or outcome occurred.

Impact of Covid

The concept of reasonableness during the time of Covid may act as mitigation for the Defendant if it can show that decisions taken or not taken were in accordance with then current government guidance. Priorities had to be made so would a respectable body of medical opinion have acted similarly? This was a worldwide healthcare crisis with a virus that was largely unknown even in medical communities and risks of transmissibility were uncertain (at least in the initial stages). So decisions taken in this context may be deemed reasonable even if they would not have been in more certain and less pressurised times. Courts may be more sympathetic to Defendants as a result.

Context was important in *Knight v Home Office*[43] in determining the standard of care where the Court judged that standards of treatment cannot be fixed but may vary dependant on the type of hospital. This principle could be extended as between infection control standards as between a hospital and Care home.

A similar corollary may be derived from the case of *Wilsher v Essex Health Authority*.[44] The same standard of care applies between junior and more experienced clinicians without regard to experience and qualifications. This does however apply to the position occupied and allows for some consideration to be given to different skill levels. So inexperience is no defence – at least in normal times. But the pandemic was far from normal. *Wilsher* laid down the authority that normal standards apply during '*emergency or battle conditions*'. The leading judge, Mustill J did however say that '*an emergency may overburden resources and, if an individual is forced by circumstances to do too many things at once, the fact he does one of them incorrectly should not lightly be taken as negligence*'.

43 [1990] 3 All ER 237

44 [1988] AC 1074

Wilsher remains good law and has been reiterated in cases like *FB v Rana*[45] that the standard owed by doctors '*is not tailored to their individual strengths and weaknesses*'.

That should not be read as providing an immunity to healthcare staff for decisions or omissions of treatment or delays in diagnosis or contraction of Covid, for example. But the Courts do recognise and are influenced by the circumstances in which duties are performed.

As far back as 1954, Lord Denning said in *Roe v Minister for* Health[46] '*a proper sense of proportion requires us to have regard to the conditions in which doctors and hospitals have to work. We must insist on due care for the patient at every point, but we must not condemn as negligence that which is only a misadventure*'.

The *Bolam* test does have flexibility so the state of knowledge at the relevant time will be examined and the Courts will ask 'whether a reasonable body of professionals would have acted in the same way?'

The flexibility lies in appreciating how staff are deployed in times of crisis and understaffing so as to maintain the safety of staff and residents. Does this apply to staff who do work for which they are not skilled or qualified? Highly unlikely but considerations of risk and benefit will be weighed by the Court. Lack of resources is generally not a relevant factor in determining whether a Defendant has exercised reasonable care. So lack of PPE for want of funding is unlikely to impress a Court if someone catches Covid owing to a lack of face masks, for example.

Context is key was confirmed in *Mulholland v Medway NHS Foundation Trust*.[47] Whether a nurse acted reasonably and

[45] [2017] EWCA Civ 334

[46] [1954] 2 QB 66

[47] [2015] EWCA 268(QB)

professionally was considered in this case. Of relevance was the fact that it was a busy emergency department. The judge said: *'In forming a conclusion about the conduct of a practitioner working within triage within an A&E department context cannot be ignored. The assessment of breach of duty is not an abstract exercise but one formed within a context – which here is that of a busy A&E where the task of the triaging nurse is to make a quick judgment call as to where next to send the patient'.*

In determining the standard of care, the court stated it *'mist be calibrated in a manner reflecting reality'.*

One may find defendants relying on comments made by Mustill J about 'battle conditions' in situations whereby staff are overfaced by emergencies at the height of the Covid pandemic. Issues may have arisen where nurses have been redeployed to a different Care home and are therefore unfamiliar with work practices and systems at the new home.

The impact of Covid has been tested in the reported clinical negligence claim of *Sanderson v Guy's and St Thomas' NHS Foundation Trust*[48] concerning delays in fetal monitoring and birth injury. The Court found no negligence holding that the environment of care was a relevant factor to consider. Mrs Justice Lambert stated: *'The fact that nurses and doctors and others are working in a 'war zone' with Covid-19 in unfamiliar clinical environments, means that the care context cannot, in my view, be ignored'.*

This case also explored the use of clinical guidelines that the Court found to be limited. They did not provide a substitute for clinical judgement. Therefore if some clinicians do not observe the NICE Guidelines then failure to do so is not *Bolam* negligent.

---

48 [2020] EWHC 20 (QB)

Priorities were explored in *Morrison v Liverpool Women's NHS Foundation Trust*[49] where there was an issue as to possible competing priorities where there was alleged delay in performing a caesarean section and whether that was *Bolam* negligent. Although the Recorder at first instance – finding for the Claimant – did not refer to the *Bolam/Bolitho* tests, Turner J, who dismissed the appeal, considered that the test was correctly applied. Interestingly the appeal judge was not critical of the Claimant's expert's failure to point to literature or guidance to support his conclusions, nor for that matter did the Defendant's expert do so either. The court recognised that it would be 'mechanistic' to conclude that the absence of published material where there were a 'limitless number of permutations' would be insurmountable to a finding of breach of duty. Although the events in this case preceded Covid, Turner J recognised the pressures on clinicians when he stated:

> '*…in the clinical context a balance has to be struck between the needs of any given patient and any other competing professional demands placed upon the clinicians involved. Sometimes, the seriousness and urgency of a patient's presentation and the absence of any conflicting factors will mandate a swift and decisive response. On other occasions, it is equally obvious that the needs of the patient must be deprioritised to allow the clinicians to attend other demands on their time of as a matter priority*'.

He went on to say that where the risk to the patient was sufficiently low then postponement of treatment would be justified. In this case, the first instance judge (reasonably) did not find there were any competing considerations, with no evidence called by the Defendant to support his suggestion that there were such other priorities.

The pandemic will have created intense pressures, and priorities are likely to be relevant but evidence will be necessary to rebut a Claimant's

49 [2020] EWHC 91 (QB)

allegations on delay. However, in certain circumstances, a Claimant will have received the undivided attention of the clinician and while Covid may be the cause of injury or death, it may be caused by straightforward negligence, and then the pandemic should not be allowed to sully the waters. The standard of care remains unaffected, as judged by the specialism rather than the clinician's seniority or experience.

NHS Resources will feature in Covid litigation and may also apply to that of Care Homes too where they receive public funding either from the NHS or Local Authorities. This is linked to priorities we suggest. The Courts may have regard to non-clinical reasons for delays when assessing reasonableness. In *University College London Hospitals NHS Foundation Trust v MB*[50] that involved a claim by the NHS against a patient who was refusing to leave their hospital bed, the Court examined the allocation of resources set against the patient's human rights under Article 3 ECHR. The judge in considering whether the Trust's application for an injunction requiring the patient to vacate their hospital bed should be granted reflected on the allocation of 'scarce public resources'. It featured in his consideration as to whether there was a breach of human rights.

One could see the Courts making assessments on breach of duty in clinical negligence claims reflecting the acute financial and logistical difficulties during the pandemic. A pivotal question is whether the courts will effectively make an assessment reflecting a lower, albeit objective standard of care. Each case is of course fact specific so no generalisations can be made but the evidence so far of the limited clinical negligence cases reported is that no real adjustment has been made.

---

50 [2020] EWHC 882 (QB)

Limitation

There is a period of 3 years to bring proceedings for a personal injury and clinical negligence claim[51] from the date the cause of action accrued or the date of knowledge, if later. This could be a problem if the Claimant has not already made arrangements for a moratorium on limitation or agreed an extension of time as they could be out of time. Let us suppose the Claimant sustained Covid-19 in March 2020, then they must have issued proceedings by March 2023 otherwise they are out of time and statute barred. If solicitors have been instructed and the claim pursued, an extension should have been agreed. Those solicitors may have obtained an automatic extension if they are members of AvMA or SCIL (by virtue of the Covid-19 Clinical Negligence Protocol 2020, now updated to the Clinical Negligence Claims Agreement 2024). This is mentioned in chapter 6.1. Limitation may not be a problem if the Claimant is a protected party, such as where they lack capacity, otherwise known as being under a disability at the time they sustained Covid. This is because 3 years does not run until they cease to be under a disability[52]. There may be arguments that a Claimant did not gain knowledge that contraction of Covid was attributable to any negligence until much later.

5.2 STATUTORY DUTY

There are a panoply of statutory regulations that affect Care home providers and their relevance will be determined by the potential wrongs that are being explored and the identity of the parties. So for example there are the primary duties owed by the State, Care homes and hospitals to residents, patients, employees and visitors. The relationship between employer and employee is relevant in an

[51] Section 11(4) Limitation Act 1980

[52] Section 28 Limitation Act 1980

employers' liability claim. This could be brought either as a personal injury claim or in clinical negligence e.g. the former for failing to provide a safe work environment and/or a failure to provide adequate PPE. A claim could be brought by a visitor under *The Occupiers' Liability Act*, an employee under *The Health and Safety at Work Act 1974* and *one of the six-pack regulations*, while a service user (care home resident) has the protection of *The Health and Social Care Act 2008* and the associated 2014 regulations together with *The Care Act 2014.*

An Act that is not well known but may be relevant in circumscribing a duty of care (whether in negligence or statutory duty) – particularly in times of national emergency – is *The Social Action, Responsibility and Heroism Act 2015* (Sarah Act). This may place into context the impact of the pandemic. At the bill reading stage, the opposition Labour Party at the time described it as a 'vacuous waste of time'. Courts do have a duty to consider its provisions but it will not be displacing the standard tests on breach of duty. It applies where someone has acted for the benefit of society or demonstrated a predominantly responsible approach towards protecting the safety of others or acted heroically by intervening in an emergency. The exceptional circumstances arising during the pandemic may in fact find a place for 'Sarah' after all.

A country cousin is *The Compensation Act 2006* which provides that when considering breach of duty, the Courts should consider whether the steps necessary to comply with the duty of care may prevent a desirable activity from being undertaken at all. Clearly healthcare is more than desirable and in the context of Covid, it is crucial, so this Act may have limited applicability. It does underline however that the standard of care does have limits.

The three potential Claimants are now considered. They are residents (service users), employees and visitors.

(a) Service users

A care home is defined by s.3 *Care Standards Act 2000* to premises where residents occupy their rooms on a licence. The Act provides for regulation of agencies and providers to ensure their competence in discharge of the duty of care. Five principles were at the heart of the Act: dignity and respect, compassion, responsive care and support and wellbeing. It was superseded in England by the *The Health and Social Care Act* 2008 although the former Act still regulates adult social care in Wales. The 2008 Act has 6 Parts. Part 3 Section 2 provides for Regulations setting out the fundamental standards. They are encapsulated in a Statutory Instrument – *Health and Social Care Act 2008 (Regulated Activities) Regulations 2014*. They are:

- Reg 9 Person-centred care
- Reg 10 Dignity and respect
- Reg 11 Need for consent
- Reg 12 Safe care and treatment
- Reg 13 Safeguarding service users from abuse and improper treatment
- Reg 14 Meeting nutritional and hydration needs
- Reg 15 Premises and equipment
- Reg 16 Receiving and acting on complaints
- Reg 17 Good governance
- Reg 18 Staffing

- Reg 19 Fit and proper persons employed
- Reg 20 Duty of candour

Regulations 9,10,12,13 and 17 have particular pertinence to claims arising out of Covid. They are linked to and effectively incorporate aspects of the HRA.

So Regulations 9 (Person-centred care) and 10 (Dignity and respect) reflect Article 8 Respect for private and family life. This might apply for example to a restriction on visitors to care homes.

Regulation 12 (Safe care and treatment) covered by Article 2 Right to life; this could apply where there is a failure to provide appropriate and safe care, or where there was a restriction on food and fluid.

Regulation 13 (Safeguarding) would apply to Article 3 Freedom of torture and inhuman or degrading treatment. This could apply where there is a failure to safeguard from harm. Also applies to Article 5 Right to liberty and security. This would include seclusion of residents for long periods of time without review; Or excessive use of medication, restricting movement.

Regulation 15 (Premises and equipment) covers cleanliness (including decontamination) of premises and suitability for their intended purpose. It would apply to the layout of care homes that do not have sufficient safe movement areas or segregation for those with Covid symptoms or perhaps discharged from hospital. It includes provision of appropriate information on access and entry especially where restrictions are in place.

Regulation 17 (Good governance) would apply to all Articles where systemic failures of leadership failed to provide governance for a rights-based culture.

Of all the Regulations perhaps **Regulation 12** applies with most force to the care home environment. This requires that risks to health and safety during any care or treatment be assessed. Premises and equipment must be safe and in sufficient quantities. Providers must prevent and control the spread of infection. Given its significance Regulation 12 is set out here:

1. Care and treatment must be provided in a safe way for service users.

2. Without limiting paragraph (1), the things which a registered person must do to comply with that paragraph include

   (a) assessing the risks to the health and safety of service users of receiving the care or treatment;

   (b) doing all that is reasonably practicable to mitigate any such risks;

   (c) ensuring that persons providing care or treatment to service users have the qualifications, competence, skills and experience to do so safely;

   (d) ensuring that the premises used by the service provider are safe to use for their intended purpose and are used in a safe way;

   (e) ensuring that the equipment used by the service provider for providing care or treatment to a service user is safe for such use and is used in a safe way;

   (f) where equipment or medicines are supplied by the service provider, ensuring that there are sufficient quantities of these to ensure the safety of service users and to meet their needs;

   (g) the proper and safe management of medicines;

(h) assessing the risk of, and preventing, detecting and controlling the spread of, infections, including those that are health care associated;

(i) where responsibility for the care and treatment of service users is shared with, or transferred to, other persons, working with such other persons, service users and other appropriate persons to ensure that timely care planning takes place to ensure the health, safety and welfare of the service users.

The Guidance and the Code of Practice on the prevention and control of infections and related guidance published by the Department of Health and Social Care in 2015 and refreshed in December 2022. The update takes account of changes wrought by Covid.

Organisations like Care homes and NHS bodies must have in place policies, procedures and protocols to deal with infection control. The code now reflects the changes necessary to comply with *The Health and Social Care Act 2008 (Regulated Activities) Regulations 2014* and the role of infection prevention. Significantly the code is not mandatory if a provider can demonstrate that it meets the regulations in a different way. There are 10 compliance criteria against which standards will be judged:

Criterion 1 – Systems to manage and monitor the prevention and control of infection, e.g. risk assessments and susceptibility of residents and risks posed by their environment and by other residents.

Criterion 2 – The provision and maintenance of a clean and appropriate environment facilitating the prevention and control of infections.

Criterion 3 – Appropriate antimicrobial use.

Criterion 4 – The provision of information on infections to residents, visitors and anyone else providing support or nursing/medical care.

Criterion 5 – A policy of identifying those who are at risk of infection promptly and receive treatment and care to reduce the risk of transmission of infection to other people.

Criterion 6 – Systems in place to ensure that all care workers (including contractors and care workers) discharge their responsibilities in the process of preventing and controlling infection.

Criterion 7 – The ability to secure adequate isolation facilities.

Criterion 8 – The ability to secure adequate access to laboratory support as appropriate.

Criterion 9 – Policies designed for the resident's care that will help to prevent and control infections.

Criterion 10 – Systems to manage staff health and wellbeing with an organisational obligation to manage infection, prevention and control.

The *Care Act 2014* proscribes the duties that Local authorities owe to those receiving services and is essentially one of a safeguarding role and ensuring the promotion of wellbeing. Underpinning this is the provision of information. In an action against a Local Authority this act may well be relevant though it was watered down by the *Coronavirus Act 2020.* If a Local Authority provided funding and/or owned a care home then it is suggested that the 2008 act and its 2014 regulations will be more relevant.

(b) Employees

Employers owe duties to their staff for their health and welfare both under the common law in negligence but also statutory duties under the *Health and Safety at Work Act 1974* (HSW). Section 2 of the HSW requires the employer to take measures to prevent the risk of employees' exposure to Covid-19. That may, for example, include social distancing and segregation. Subordinate legislation in the form of the 'six-pack' regulations set out obligations on an employer to institute an appropriate assessment of workplace risk, monitoring of workplace health and safety, and providing information and training as to risks and risk avoidance. Statutory duties represent evidence of good practice that a reasonable employer should adopt.

Previously many breaches of the 'six-pack regulations' imposed strict liability by reason of section 47(2) HSW. The *Enterprise and Regulatory Reform Act 2013* (ERRA) removed any civil liability from the HSW (although strangely criminal sanctions remained). But breach of any of the workplace regulations whilst not creating a liability in itself, does mean that Claimants may rely upon any failures as actions or omissions that constitute negligence. So it is back to the common law. Reliance on negligence under the old regime was not always necessary. Nevertheless it remains desirable to explore the regulations underpinning the workplace relationship in order to plead breach of statutory duty. It was thought that when the ERRA came out (for accidents after 1st October 2013) that claims in employers' liability (EL) would be severely compromised in circumstances hitherto when it was perceived as easier to succeed as a Claimant under statutory duty (because of strict liability) rather than in negligence. The perception being that unmeritorious cases were successful at the cost of a largely 'innocent' employer. Presumably the inference being that the Claimant was in some way not the injured party or at least was less innocent than the overburdened employer. But as ever, the Claimant has the burden of proving their case on breach, foreseeability, causation and loss. Defendants always have been able to plead no 'reasonable practicability' in controlling or reducing a risk that eventuated. It has always been about assessment of risk so strict liability as applied was always qualified.

But there is a valid argument to say that there is now a greater emphasis on expert evidence for the employee to show what steps could or should have been taken in answer to the reasonable practicability point.

It was always thus that claims would be pleaded under both heads and this remains the case but the emphasis has changed, although not as dramatically as originally anticipated.

Interestingly the 'Six-pack' regulations emanate from Europe – the European Directives and so it could be argued (not always successfully) that where the Defendant is an emanation of the state, then direct effect applies, thus escaping ERRA. In a claim against a public body which will include care homes run by local authorities, it may be helpful to plead not only breach of the Regulation but also the relevant Directive as it may not be fully incorporated into UK law. Indeed this was the situation in the case of *Wetherell v Student Loans Company Limited*[53] that was a personal injury claim concerning hearing loss. Expert evidence opined that the headset provided by the employer, the Student Loans Company complied with all relevant health and safety regulations. A claim under PUWER and therefore negligence would not succeed so the twin EU Directive – the *Work Equipment (the Second) Directive 89/655* (now 2009/104/EC) was pursued. The burden lay on the Defendant (ERRA did not apply to an EU Directive) to prove that the injury resulted from unforeseeable circumstances beyond its control. The Claimant failed at first instance before HHJ Freedman holding that the SLC was not an emanation of the state. Likewise, on appeal before Eyre J the same findings applied.

So here are the 'Six-pack' – actually there are seven EL regulations, the seventh arriving a little later, namely COSHH.

- *Provision and Use of Work Equipment Regulations 1992/1999* (PUWER)

---

53 [2024] EWHC 1443 (KB)

- *Manual Handling Operations Regulations 1992* (MHOR)
- *Personal Protective Equipment at Work Regulations 1992/2022* (PPE)
- *Workplace (Health, Safety and Welfare) Regulations 1992* (WHSWR)
- *Health and Safety (Display Screen Equipment) Regulations 1992* (HSDSER)
- *Management of Health and Safety at Work Regulations 1993/1999* (MHSWR)
- *Control of Substances Hazardous to Health Regulations 1994/1998* (COSHH)

The main EL regulations that are likely to apply in the Care home environment concerning Covid are PUWER, PPE.

❖ PUWER

Reg 4

(1) Every employer shall ensure that work equipment is so constructed or adapted as to be suitable for the purpose for which it is used or provided.

(2) In selecting work equipment, every employer shall have regard to the working conditions and to the risks to the health and safety of persons which exist in the premises or undertaking in which that work equipment is to be used and any additional risk posed by the use of that work equipment.

Examples of work equipment include wheelchair, walking aids, hoists and adjustable height baths.

Service users might be carried, or aided into a hydraulic lift bed. Lifting equipment may be governed by the *Lifting Operations and Lifting Equipment Regulations 1998.* There is also an obvious overlap with PPE. However PUWER deals with general considerations of health and safety, so addressing the risk of accidental injury. Contrast with PPE which is designed to protect against a particular risk or hazard that is known about.

❖ MHOR

Manual handling can be a frequent cause of injuries in the care sector (moving a resident?), although not particularly specific to Covid. A manual handling operation is defined in Regulation 2 as:

> *"'Manual handling operations' means any transporting or supporting of a load (including the lifting, putting down, pushing, pulling, carrying or moving thereof) by hand or bodily force."*

Reg 4(1) sets out the duties of an employer:

> *(a) so far as is reasonably practicable, avoid the need for his employees to undertake any manual handling operations at work which involve a risk of their being injured; or*
>
> *(b) where it is not reasonably practicable to avoid the need for his employees to undertake any manual handling operations at work which involve a risk of their being injured –*
>
> > *(i) make a suitable and sufficient assessment of all such manual handling operations to be undertaken by them, having regard to the factors which are specified in column 1 of Schedule 1 to these Regulations and*

considering the questions which are specified in the corresponding entry in column 2 of that Schedule.

Schedule 1 addresses the nature of the task; the weight of the load and how easy it is to grasp; the working environment; capability of person doing the moving; and other factors such as restrictions on movement or posture by protective clothing, for example

(ii) take appropriate steps to reduce the risk of injury to those employees arising out of their undertaking any such manual handling operations to the lowest level reasonable practicable, and

(iii) take appropriate steps to provide any of those employees who are undertaking any such manual handling operations with general indications and, where it is reasonably practicable to do so, precise information on –

(aa) the weight of each load, and

(bb) the heaviest side of any load whose centre of gravity is not positioned centrally.

A failure of an employer to carry out a risk assessment of itself will not be sufficient to establish liability, unless the failure is of causal significance to the injury. In assessing an employer's lack of care, failure to comply with Regulation 4 will contribute to a finding of negligence.

❖ PPE

Initially this afforded protection to employees, defined as working under an employment contract ('limb (a) workers'). It was extended on 6 April 2022 to those who have a more casual working relationship, working under a contract for service ('limb (b) workers'). In the care industry limb (b) workers could be particularly prevalent.

Reg 4(1) & (2) [abridged]:

> '(1) *Every employer shall ensure that suitable personal protective equipment is provided to his employees who may be exposed to a risk to their health or safety while at work except where and to the extent that such risk has been adequately controlled by other means which are equally or more effective*
>
> *(2), personal protective equipment shall not be suitable unless-*
>
> > *(a) it is appropriate for the risks involved, the conditions at the place where exposure to the risk may occur, and the period for which it is worn;*
> >
> > *(d) so far as is practicable, it is effective to prevent or adequately control the risk or risks involved without increasing overall risk.*

PPE guidance for staff

The government first issued guidance to those working in care homes on 17 April 2020 (see 'How to work Safely in Care Homes'); this was updated in July 2020. It should be read in conjunction with the NICE guidelines on standard infection prevention and control precautions;[54] Public Health England's (PHE) guidance on the use of PPE; and the Health and Safety Executive.[55]

A care worker providing close personal care such as touching or coming within 2 metres of a resident who is coughing must wear disposable gloves, a disposable plastic apron, a fluid-repellent (Type IIR) surgical mask and eye protection.

---

54 www.nice.org.uk/guidance/cg139

55 'Personal Protective Equipment ('PPE') at Work, INDG174

If no personal care was being provided at the time and there was no one else within 2 metres that had a cough, then the recommendations differed in that only a Type II surgical mask was required. In July 2020 there was an update to include a third situation; namely exceeding 2 metres, where a Type I or Type II surgical mask could be used continuously by a member of staff.

The guidance emphasised that PPE was only effective when combined with

- hand hygiene
- respiratory hygiene ('catch it, bin it, kill it') and avoidance of touching face
- infection prevention and control procedures
- correct procedure for putting on and taking off PPE and
- safe disposal of used PPE.

On 24 April 2020, PHE issued revised guidance on the use of PPE in the health and social care industries. It stated that:

- Aprons and gloves to be single patient use;
- Certain respirators, fluid resistant masks, eye protection and disposable coveralls could be used during a single session in certain circumstances;
- PPE may need to be changed according to different circumstances during a single care episode;
- No evidence then existed that disposal of respirators, facemasks or eye protection between each patient reduced the risk of

infection transmission. Actual frequent handling could increase the risk of exposure;

- PPE should not be single use where damaged, soiled, compromised or uncomfortable;

- As to be determined by the care worker, if a risk to themselves or a service user, then they should wear a fluid repellent surgical mask with or without eye protection;

- Disposable aprons are subject to single use;

- Disposable fluid repellent coveralls or long sleeved gowns for single or single session use;

- Disposable gloves to be worn during direct patient care and with exposure to blood or other body fluids, and then disposed after single use.

In reviewing whether PPE was effective, was it 'suitable' within Regulation 4(3)? Was it appropriate for the risks and conditions involved. Did the mask fit correctly? Was it effective in controlling the risk. It was not adequate to simply provide masks, aprons, gloves etc. and presume that a care worker would use appropriately. Proper training should have been given and documented.

Private care homes were responsible for purchasing their own PPE. Did they purchase sufficient of the correct specification? Were they re-using equipment. Was it available only for certain members of staff?

Regulation 10 provides that there must be monitoring of exposure of employees to Covid-19 and records maintained and available for perusal.

Given that all care workers in a care home are liable to be exposed to Covid, then Regulation 11 stipulates that they should be kept under suitable health surveillance, with record keeping.

❖ WHSWR

This applies to the structure and layout of a building and provision of services, for example, the layout of traffic routes, seating and rest facilities. It may apply where a care worker trips because of a crowded corridor obstructed by cleaning facilities or a wheelchair, making an inadequate pedestrian route. These regulations apply not only to employers but also to co-workers, the self-employed and to visitors. The salient regulations to consider are:

Reg 5 – the workplace is to be maintained in an efficient state, in efficient working order and in good repair.

Reg 12 – covers floor and traffic routes, both pedestrian and vehicular, including stairs, ladders and doorways.

Reg 13 – concerns prevention of falls. Measures must be 'suitable and effective' and 'reasonably practicable' to avoid falling a distance or being struck by an object.

Reg 17 – deals with the layout of traffic routes, creating a demarcation between pedestrians and vehicles.

❖ MHSWR

These Regulations are all about risk assessments.

Reg 3 – an employer must carry out a suitable and sufficient risk assessment to the health and safety of employees whilst at work.

Reg 4 – where preventative and protective measures are applied, risks must be evaluated and prevented, following liason with employees. There is a duty to warn and tailor advice dependant on category of worker and risk profile.

❖ COSHH

Reg 6:

> '(1) *An employer shall not carry out work which is liable to expose any employees to any substance hazardous to health unless he has –*
>
> (a) *made a suitable and sufficient assessment of the risk created by that work to the health of those employees and of the steps that need to be taken to meet the requirements of these Regulations; and*
>
> (b) *implemented the steps referred to in sub-paragraph (a)*'

A risk assessment should have been carried out in a Care home about management of Covid infections and how to reduce or avoid them. Control measures must have been instituted. The HSE refers to specific micro-organisms and diseases such as influenza, Legionella, Anthrax and BSE but clearly coronaviruses apply as it will constitute a biological agent under regulation 2. COSHH does not apply where one employee catches a respiratory infection from another or a member of the public has infected an employee with coronavirus through general transmission in a non-health related workplace. But it does apply to employees who care for infectious patients, so will apply to care workers. Employer's duties also extend to third parties such as visitors.

So what should a care home have undertaken in its risk assessment?

- The hazardous properties of Covid-19;

- The level, type and duration of any employee's exposure to Covid-19;
- The circumstances of the work undertaken by the health care worker;
- Any additional circumstances that give risk to a high risk of exposure (e.g. non-availability of PPE)
- The effect of any preventative and control measures that have been, or will be, taken
- The results of 'health surveillance'
- The results of monitoring of exposure;
- Any further information the employer requires in order to complete the assessment (e.g. limitations on cross-infection control measures as a result of limited availability of PPE).

Reg 7:

> '(1) *Every employer shall ensure that the exposure of his employees to a substance hazardous to health is either prevented or, where this is not reasonably practicable, adequately controlled'*
>
> *'In this regulation 'adequate' means adequate having regard only to the nature of the substance and the nature and degree of exposure to substances hazardous to health and 'adequately' shall be construed accordingly.'*

Regulation 7 requires the employer to design and use work systems to minimise exposure to Covid-19. This may include work rotation together with sufficient protective equipment. There must have been appropriate decontamination and disinfection procedures, safe collection, storage and disposal of contaminated waste, a testing regime for Covid-19 and making vaccines available.

❖ *Employer's Liability (Defective Equipment) Act 1969*

This does not impose statutory duties and is not constrained by the ERRA so strict liability may apply where an employer is deemed negligent, i.e. subject to proving fault. Fault is wider than negligence but also includes breach of statutory duty or 'other act or omission' which gives rise to liability. The burden remains on the Claimant to prove it.

Section 1

(1) Where after the commencement of this Act –

(a) an employee suffers personal injury in the course of his employment in consequence of a defect in equipment provided by his employer for the purposes of the employer's business; and

(b) the defect is attributable wholly or partly to the fault of a third party (whether identified or not),

the injury shall be deemed to be also attributable to negligence on the part of the employer (whether or not he is liable in respect of the injury apart from this subsection), but without prejudice to the law relating to contributory negligence and to any remedy by way of contribution or in contract or otherwise which is available to the employer in respect of the injury.

Not dissimilar in import to the ELA is the *Consumer Protection Act 1987* (CPA) that also creates a form of strict liability. No proof of fault is required. No statutory duties apply. It is sufficient to establish existence of a 'defect' in a product.

(c) Visitors

Occupiers' liability describes the duties owed by owners of the premises or having control over them to people who enter the property. The duty is imposed by virtue of the *Occupiers' Liability Act* 1957. It was updated in 1984 to include lawful trespassers but that revision is unlikely to apply to visitors of care homes.

The most likely visitor could be a family relation or friend of a resident in a care home (when visiting was permitted) or it may be someone contracted to undertake work on the premises or someone making a delivery. In times of Covid, they put themselves at greater risk by visiting a care home. If they contracted coronavirus because of exposure to someone infected in a care home, there may be grounds for bringing a public liability claim (PL). Evidence to explore a claim may include requesting PPE training records, use of PPE, cleaning processes, risk registers/assessments, details of previous Covid outbreaks and how managed, care plans and testing regimes; review of visiting rotas and cohorting staff teams so that only the same care staff interacted where a Covid outbreak, CQC inspections, staff training records, hand sanitisers, screens, floor marking, zoning and quarantining by way of examples. Disclosure may be less than forthcoming and require a court application or at least the threat of one.

The starting point, it is suggested, is whether the care home has followed government advice and guidance and whether this had departed from expert advice or guidance issued by the WHO, for example.

The 1957 Act states:

Section 1(1) proscribes the duty owed by an occupier to a visitor:

> *'in respect of dangers due to the state of the premises or to things done or omitted to be done on them'.*

Section 2(1) addresses the scope of duty owed:

> *'An occupier of premises owes the same duty, the 'common duty of care' to all his visitors, except insofar as he is free to and does extend, restrict, modify or exclude his duty to any visitor or visitors by agreement or otherwise'.*

Section 2(2) defines the common duty of care as one that is *reasonable* in all the circumstances for the purposes for which the visitor is invited or permitted to be there. The common duty of care varies according to the circumstances. A care home with vulnerable residents who may carry Covid will be fixed with a higher standard of care than someone visiting a private house.

That said one of the main difficulties for a visitor who contracts Covid and believes they were exposed to an infectious person in a care home is to prove factual causation. Given the prevalence of coronavirus in the population at the high point, a Court will require some persuasion that transfer occurred during a visit, unless there was an obvious point of transmission or no other possible contact points.

Another difficulty could be an argument raised by a Defendant of 'volenti non fit injuria' ('voluntary assumption of risk'). This would be raised on the basis that the visitor appreciated that there was an increased risk of attending a care home during the pandemic. Although a possibility, it is difficult to see a Court being impressed by such an argument given the circumstances upon which a visitor would be attending a care home to see a relative and the expectation that very high standards of cleanliness and infection control would be expected. At the very least one would expect a care home to have at its entrance a protocol on admission or make it known to visitors by prior appointment. Visitors should be issued with protective clothing and especially masks. Physical distancing should be mandatory and the number of visitors strictly controlled.

Ultimately it will be down to the due diligence of the property owners/managers and the existence and deployment of systems to protect or reduce Covid transmission. It may have meant that visitors should have been refused entry because the risks were too great given the number of infections that may have been present in a care home.

5.3 CONTRACT

This applies to where a resident pays privately for their care home fees. Self-funded care home residents pay for their care when their savings or income exceeds the threshold. It may be organised by themselves or through the local authority. Those people who receive care in a charity-run care home are also defined as self-funders. It is possible that some residents may receive NHS-funded nursing care in a care home despite being self-funders.

The point is that those who pay or make a financial contribution towards their care will have a contract with the care home. And that care home owes a contractual duty of care. In many situations the standard of the duty owed will be the same as that in the tort of negligence. But it may affect the remedy claimed of damages, especially if one were seeking to recover some or all of the fees paid to the care home. Given that the care home will have provided consideration in the form of accommodation, food and service, it is highly unlikely that full fees would be recoverable. Much depends on the nature of the contract between provider and resident. For example if representations have been made about a higher standard of care then it is arguable that the minimal *Bolam* standard does not apply.

Some courts are loath to make findings of breach of contract against an individual clinician unless she has made particular statements over and above the expected standard of care. Damages resultant from a finding of breach of contract may be awarded to place the Claimant in the financial position that he or she would have been in had there been full performance of the agreement.

Caution needs to be exercised in reviewing the status of healthcare providers and whether they are employed by the care home or are classified as independent contractors. For the most part it will be expected that clinicians will be employed by a care home and therefore any acts or omissions by them under the principle of vicarious liability will render the care home liable for their breaches. But should staff be engaged as independent contractors, such as a visiting doctor or nurse engaged on a private basis, then regard must be had as to whether they are a party to any proceedings. It could be that the care home in that situation may deny owing a non-delegable duty to the Claimant[56]. There would need to be an examination as to whether the clinician providing care was employed under an employment contract or whether that person arranged payment of his own tax, National Insurance, professional indemnity insurance etc, and whether he or she provided services elsewhere.

5.4 HUMAN RIGHTS ACT

Application to Care Homes

This is the fourth element that should be considered in formulating the cause of action and may be applicable to where the Defendant is a public authority or even a private care home provider.

There is a broad definition as to whether an organisation constitutes a 'public authority' and it is set out in sections 6(3) to 6(6) HRA. Central

56 See *Hughes v Rattan* [2022] EWCA Civ 107 on principles of delegable duty. Here, the Court of Appeal held that a dental practice did owe NHS patients a non-delegable duty for treatment provided by independent contractor Dentists.

and local government are 'core' public authorities and are liable for **all** of their actions where incompatible with the ECHR. There are two exceptions – where they could not have acted any differently because of primary legislation OR legislation cannot be interpreted to be compatible with the ECHR and the authority acted to enforce those provisions.

The delivery of residential care services amounts to a public function for the purposes of the HRA by reason of *s145 Health and Social Care Act 2008*. This provides that a person who provides accommodation, together with nursing or personal care, in a care home for an individual is to be taken to be exercising a public function if the services are provided under statutory arrangements, i.e. provided or arranged by local authorities. This means that such a Care home will be bound by s.6 of the HRA.

Hybrid public authorities are more problematical. A private body may be regarded as a public authority for the purposes of the HRA if it performs *'functions of a public nature'* It is the functions they perform that is relevant rather than the nature of the organisation.

However there will be no dilemma as regards the Secretary of State for Health– they will be captured by s6 HRA.

A claim for damages may be brought under section 73 *Care Act 2014*.

Privately run Care homes are not a core public authority for the purpose of section 6 HRA. They are not hybrid public authorities either as they do not fall within s.73 of the *Care Act.* This applies where registered care providers either provide personal care to adults in their home, or accommodation with nursing or personal care, which has been arranged or funded by a public authority, are exercising a function of a public nature for the purposes of the HRA 1998. The recent case of *Sammut v Next Steps Mental Healthcare Ltd and Greater Manchester*

Mental Health Foundation Trust[57] confirms the position. Even if the private nursing home were a public or hybrid authority (which it was not), on the facts, Article 2 was not engaged. As HHJ Bird said the alleged breach of Article 2 was in reality no more than an allegation of (very serious) clinical negligence outwith the scope of Article 2. Recklessness as to the risk to life as a result of denial of treatment was insufficient to engage Article 2. It is the need for 'full awareness' to elevate above clinical negligence.

Who may bring a claim

The Claimant must be a victim of an unlawful act or would be a victim of any proposed unlawful act in order to bring a claim under the HRA (*s.7(1)(b) HRA).* A direct victim is clearly the injured party. An indirect victim for the purposes of *Article 2* violations will be either the deceased's next-of-kin representing the estate (Executor/Executrix or Personal Representative); or a blood relative, spouse or partner for their own pain, distress and bereavement at the treatment of the deceased leading to their death. Those who are indirect victims must be listed in the Claim in their own right in addition to the estate.

A separate claim to that of tort would apply where potential Claimants (such as parents) would not be able to bring a negligence claim arising from the death of their adult son or daughter in a care home. *Rabone and another v Pennine Care NHS Foundation Trust* [2012] UKSC 2 established that the parents of the deceased were entitled to bring their own ECHR article 2 claim arising from their daughter's suicide, which resulted from the trust's failure to meet its article 2 obligations to protect her from this real and immediate risk.

Rabone was applied in *Daniel and another v St George's Healthcare Trust & London Ambulance Service* [2016] EWHC 23 (QB) sets out the issues in determining 'victim status', namely:

57 [2024] EWHC 2265(KB)

1. The nature of the legal/family relationship between the Claimants and the deceased;

2. The nature of the personal ties between the Claimants and the deceased;

3. The extent to which violation of the ECHR affected them personally; and

4. Involvement in the proceedings arising out of the deceased's death.

Here, the Claimants were the foster mother and foster brother of the deceased who died in prison from a heart attack. The central allegations concerned delay in summoning an ambulance and its dispatch. The claim was brought alleging that both Defendants were public authorities and as such acted in breach of Articles 2 and 3 of the ECHR. The first Claimant, foster mother succeeded in establishing herself as an indirect victim; she had been the foster mother for 3 years leading to a longstanding parent-child relationship. The second Claimant failed in his claim as found not to be an indirect victim. The status of 'foster brother' is not recognised in UK domestic law nor in ECHR case law. Further he was a young child when the deceased was fostered and their relationship was more akin to '*…a close friendship between childhood school friends or family friends*'.

Thus in order for a person to have 'suffered gravely' they must have a family tie or have some legal relationship with the deceased.

Cases in the ECHR recognise that family members can also be 'direct victims' of treatment contrary to article 3 on account of the suffering stemming from serious human rights violations affecting their relatives – see *Janowiec and others v Russia* App Nos 55508/07 and 29520/09, 21 October 2013. The principles are set out at para 177:

> *The Court has always been sensitive in its case law to the profound psychological impact of a serious human rights violation on the victim's family members who are applicants before the court. However in order for a separate violation of article 3 of the ECHR to be found in respect of the victim's relatives, there should be special factors in place giving their suffering a dimension and character distinct from the emotional distress inevitably stemming from the aforementioned violation itself. The relevant factors include the proximity of the family tie, the particular circumstances of the relationship, the extent to which the family member witnessed the events in question and the involvement of the applicants in the attempts to obtain information about the fate of their relatives.*

The Claims

For claims against care homes, as we have seen in *Gardner,* the potentially operative Articles are 2,3,8 and 14, although realistically it will be Articles 2 (Right to life) and 8 (Right to respect for private and family life) that may be engaged. One could also include Article 5 (Right to liberty and security of person). Article 3 (Freedom from torture or inhuman or degrading treatment of punishment) is likely to be very difficult to establish in the healthcare context.

Article 2

It is the positive obligations with which we are concerned. And more especially the operational duty to take reasonable steps to protect the life of an individual where state authorities knew or ought to have known that there was a real and immediate risk to the person's life. This really applies to Article 2 where, for example, a vulnerable resident is exposed to others with symptoms of Covid-19 or in fact asymptomatic people – who have been permitted access to the care home without testing or shielding – come into contact with a vulnerable resident.

Equally it could apply to a vulnerable resident who has not received access themselves to testing or medical services.

Although we refer to 'vulnerable' residents, it could be said that by virtue of their status of being in a care home necessarily implies that all residents are 'vulnerable' to some degree as they will be infirm, aged and likely have pre-existing medical conditions.

Article 2 may apply even where someone has not lost their life but where the situation constitutes a near death situation. In examining the failure by the State in its regulatory duties, it must be shown that it operated to the patient's detriment. So even where there may be a finding of medical negligence, it does not follow that Article 2 is breached unless there is a finding that the regulatory framework failed to ensure proper protection of the patient's life. In the context of public health authorities, in certain circumstances, where an individual's life is put at risk through the denial of health care provided to the population generally may engage Article 2.[58]

In two very exceptional circumstances, the Court has accepted that Article 2 has been breached: Firstly where an individual's patient's life was knowingly put in danger by a denial of access to life-saving emergency treatment[59] and, secondly where a systemic or structural dysfunction in hospital services resulted in a patient being deprived of access to life-saving emergency treatment where the authorities knew about or ought to have known about that risk and failed to take the necessary measures to prevent that risk from materialising, this putting the patients' lives, including the life of the particular patient concerned, in danger.[60]

58 Cyprus v Turkey, 2001

59 Mehmet, Sentürk and Bekir Sentürk v Turkey, 2013

60 Aydogdu v Turkey, 2016

Although the primary duty is to protect life, the state (applied to hospitals and publically funded care homes, for example) must also have in place effective regulation of activities that may pose a risk to life. This would apply to the threat to Covid-19 in care homes and could include clear guidance and regulation on PPE requirements and access to PPE to staff and residents. It may include clear procedures around the movement of staff and residents between and in care homes and from hospitals to care homes. Was the availability of coronavirus testing kits made available to care homes and were patients tested adequately before discharge from hospital to a care home?

If there are possible violations of Article 2 the state must carry out an investigation. Here we are concerned with deaths in care homes where the Council of Europe Commissioner for Human Rights has reported on some of the problems.[61]

Article 3

The threshold for proving a claim under Article 3 is also high. To establish 'torture', ill treatment must be deliberate and cause very serious and cruel suffering. Suffering caused by negligence is unlikely to be sufficient. Inhuman treatment by contrast does not need to be intended to cause suffering. The distinction between torture and inhuman suffering is the degree of suffering caused. 'Treatment' would also include a failure to act or omission. It is possible that decision making around appropriate care and support and availability of medical treatment could potentially engage Article 3. Those are the negative obligations. The positive obligations are to protect against ill-treatment and an obligation to investigate and enforce the law. A delay in

61 'Lessons to be drawn from the ravages of the COVID-19 pandemic in long term care facilities', 20 May 2020, www.coe.int/en/web/commissioner/

diagnosis and a failure to provide medical treatment may breach Article 3 as representing inhuman and degrading treatment.[62]

Article 8

Article 8 is particularly applicable when receiving care and treatment. It includes the right to live with family, or if not, to have regular contact. So banning visitors would interfere with this right. Requiring a resident to leave a care home (which is their home) may infringe this right or restricting their movement. Similarly to Articles 2 and 3, in exceptional circumstances where a patient's life was knowingly endangered by the denial of access to treatment; or where they did not have access to treatment because of a systemic or dysfunction in hospital or a care home and the clinicians did not take the necessary measures to prevent risk happening then Article 8 may be breached. Article 8 is a qualified right so interferences may be justified as lawful where: (i) Is the restriction lawful? (ii) Does it have a legitimate aim? And (iii) Is it proportionate? Where there are wider health concerns in dealing with Covid and trying to reduce transmission to protect health would be a legitimate aim justifying certain restrictive behaviours. The same principles that apply to Article 2 also apply to Article 8 where injury falls short of threatening the right to life.

What about relatives?

It is very difficult to bring a negligence claim as a secondary victim from suffering 'nervous shock', having witnessed the death or injury of a primary victim. But the HRA provides an opening to such claims.

The issue of proximity is a bar to recovering under the common law, per *Alcock and others v Chief Constable of South Yorkshire Police* [1991] 3 WLR 1057. The House of Lords rejected negligence claims by relatives

62 Vasykov v Russia [2011] ECHR 2974/05

traumatised by watching the Hillsborough disaster unfold on television, leading to the deaths of their loved ones. It was held that this was not equivalent to being within sight and hearing of the tragedy or its immediate aftermath.

In an unreported claim involving psychological abuse of a vulnerable patient at a private hospital (reported in a *Panorama* documentary on 22 May 2019), a patient was detained under the Mental Health Act and tormented, provoked and restrained by 'carers'. The parents had no idea their daughter had been abused until they watched the Panorama footage. The decision to bring a claim under s3 HRA was based on the 'policy' decision around negligence claims for psychological injury sustained by relatives.

Relying on *Rabone,* the parents had standing to pursue a HRA claim and did so under article 3 of the ECHR. This provides an absolute prohibition on torture or inhuman or degrading treatment or punishment. As family members they were 'direct victims' of treatment contrary to article 3, per *Janowiec.* The staff at the hospital cultivated a relationship of trust and friendship with the parents who disclosed their daughters' phobias and fear of male carers when distressed. The parents were utterly devastated to see that these 'triggers' deliberately used by staff to provoke and restrain their daughter. The claim settled pre-action by way of payment of damages, an apology and costs.[63]

Interrelation with common law claims

Damages

Could claims in damages be duplicated under the common law? As Lord Hope stated in *Chester v Afshar* [2005] 1 AC 134:

[63] With recognition to gardencourtchambers.co.uk and to Legal Action Group for reproducing some of their material

> *'The function of the law is to enable rights to be vindicated and to provide remedies when duties have been breached'* and unless there is a remedy for breach of duty then the duty would become *' a hollow one, stripped of all practical force and devoid of all content'.*

So damages will be recoverable if a human right has been breached and it is governed by the severity of the breach, not by the impact of the breach on the Claimant. The award of damages is aimed principally to the upholding of standards concerning discharge of the State's (or Care Home's) duty to act in ways compatible with the Claimant's rights.

Lord Brown said in *Chief Constable of Hertfordshire Police v Van Colle* (2008) UKHL 50

> *'...convention claims have very different objectives from civil actions. Whereas civil actions are designed essentially to compensate claimants for their losses, convention claims are intended rather to uphold minimum Human Rights standards and to vindicate those rights'.*

This was stated in similar terms by Lord Bingham in *R (Greenfield) v Secretary of State for the Home Department* (2005) 1 WLR 673 by reminding the parties that s.8(3) HRA provides that no damages are to be awarded unless necessary for *'just satisfaction'.*

s.8 HRA covers remedies. They must be *'just and appropriate'* (s8(1)) and must take into account *'any other relief or remedy granted, in relation to the act in question (by that or any other court)'* (s8(3)(a)) and take into account the principles under Article 41 ECHR, vis a vis: discretion, damages are not automatic and of *'just satisfaction'.*

A Practice Direction issued by the European Court set out the principles, namely that 'just satisfaction' may be the finding of a violation itself without a compensatory award; there must be a causal link between the damage claimed and the violation found by the court; pecuniary damage will normally be awarded in full as just satisfaction and non-pecuniary damage, such as mental or physical suffering, can be compensated consistent with case law and not confined to cases with supportive medical evidence. The Court is able to infer and award compensation for distress, anxiety, frustration, injustice, prolonged uncertainty and powerlessness by reference to the nature of the violation.

There is little in the way of guidance on how to calculate quantum. There is no scale to compensate for 'just satisfaction' but it is suggested that in assessing a financial compensatory award, factors such as the nature and proximity of the familial link between the deceased and the victim, the nature of the breach and level of damage sustained by the victim – see *Rabone.*[64]

Limitation

Claims under the HRA only have 1 year to bring proceedings from the date on which the act complained of took place (s.7(5)(a)), i.e. the date of the violation. So in a fatality, this will accrue from the date of death. Compared to the standard 3 years under the common law means that time is short to investigate and prepare the claim. This applies equally to minors and protected parties, with particular relevance to the latter for our purposes. The burden is on the Claimant to bring himself within the section. Should a Defendant seek to rely upon limitation as a Defence then it must be expressly pleaded. As in the common law, there is provision to extend the time limit under s.7(5)(b) to *'such longer period as the court or tribunal considers equitable having regard to all the circumstances'.* Therefore the factors will be similar to those set out in s.33 of the Limitation Act 1980[65]. So prejudice to both parties if an extension is granted or refused; length and reasons for delay; effect of delay on the cogency of the evidence; the conduct of the Defendant after the cause of action arose; whether the Claimant acted promptly

[64] para 85

[65] para 25

when he became aware that the Defendant's acts or omissions might be capable of giving rise to an action for damages; and the steps taken by the Claimant to obtain legal or other expert advice, and the nature of the advice received.

Causation

It is generally recognised that factual causation, aka the 'but for test' that applies in negligence claims is *'looser'* in HRA claims. This is the description applied by Lord Bingham in *Greenfield:*[66]

> *'Where civil actions are designed essentially to compensate claimants for their losses, Convention claims are intended to uphold minimum human rights standards and to vindicate those rights. That is why time limits are markedly shorter…It is also why section 8(3) of the (Human Rights) Act provides that no damages are to be awarded for just satisfaction. It also seems to me to explain why a looser approach to causation is adopted under the Convention than in English tort law. Whereas the latter requires the Claimant to establish on the balance of probabilities that, but for the Defendant's negligence, he would not have suffered his claimed loss…under the Convention it appears sufficient generally to establish merely that he lost a substantial chance of this.'*

So HRA claims on causation are risk based NOT damage based. This reflected the different objectives between Convention claims intended to uphold minimum human rights standards and to provide vindication. In contrast civil claims are to compensate a Claimant for damage or loss as a consequence of negligence of the Defendant.

The case of *Sarjantson*[67] applied the risk-based approach to causation. Here the Claimant's claim under Articles 2 and 3 against the police for

66 [2005] 1WLR 673

a delayed response to a serious incident of public disorder, whereby the Claimant sustained injuries prevailed. The Court of Appeal rejected the Defendant's argument that the delay was of no consequence in that the police would not have arrived at the scene until after the Claimant had been assaulted had they been dispatched immediately. The delayed response was not relevant to liability but might affect remedy.

The test requires a Defendant to take reasonable measures to avoid an attendant risk rather than measures to eliminate the risk completely.

So if we were to extrapolate the test to the situation in a claim against a care home, the Defendant's duty in the context of Covid would be to demonstrate that measures were taken to mitigate the risk of transmission and infection. It would not be sufficient to point to systems that existed but that they were implemented. Though they would not be expected to entirely eliminate the risk of transmission.

One should examine whether a Defendant has:

- Maintained adequate screening of visitors for actual or suspected symptoms

- Separation of residents who have been discharged recently from hospital

- Isolation of residents with Covid

- Adequate treatment – transferred to hospital

[67] Sarjantson v Chief Constable of Humberside Police (2013) EWCA Civ 1252

Expert evidence

However there are advantages as expert evidence on breach of duty and causation may not be necessary, thus saving time and costs. If the claim is restricted only to a claim under human rights law, such that a public authority or care home has acted in a way that is incompatible with the Claimant's Human Rights, the expert evidence will contribute little to addressing that issue. Contrast that with a claim in negligence against a public authority that will require expert evidence.

In *Poole Borough Council v GN and another* the Supreme Court dismissed the appeal concluding that the local authority did not owe a duty of care in negligence arising out of its statutory functions to protect children from harm caused by third parties. There was no assumption of responsibility by social workers to the Claimants, although there was a contractual owed by them to the council to exercise proper professional skill and care.

5.5 JUDICIAL REVIEW

Judicial Review or JR encompasses litigation mostly in the High Court[68] (in the branch known as the Divisional Court where two justices are sitting) so as to challenge the lawfulness of a decision made by a public body, such as a government agency. Essentially it is a form of public interest litigation that act as 'checks and balances' against abuse of executive power.

JR describes the procedure by which a Claimant brings proceedings. Strictly it sits somewhat differently from the causes of actions detailed in this chapter as they represent the allegations for bringing a legal claim that are proved by breach of statute or legal precedent (the common

[68] Claims may also be brought in the Upper Tribunal such as for immigration or challenging a criminal injuries award.

law). JR is the procedure adopted to seek accountability of a public body with a view to overturning its decision on grounds of illegality, procedural unfairness and irrationality. It may require a Local authority to reverse a decision such as to provide housing, or to provide welfare benefits, for example. So to do something or not as the case may be, essentially seeking declaratory relief. To establish eligibility, a Claimant must have a 'sufficient interest' and demonstrate that internal procedures and/or alternative remedies have been exhausted.

JR is not suitable for a Claimant seeking damages against a public body like the Secretary of State for Health and Social Care, as an award is discretionary and may not be made where an alternative action was available. And a Claimant would not be able to pursue a claim against a private care home because they would not have standing. There are other difficulties, not least in funding an action; they are expensive and lawyers, it is expected, would very rarely, if at all, act on a Conditional Fee Agreement. Should the claim be lost, costs would follow the event and be payable to the Defendant. Given that the case must be brought against a public body – with the inequality of legal arms that that implies – the costs could be very substantial indeed. Additionally the limitation period for bringing a claim is only 3 months from the date that the grounds for making a claim first arose.

Therefore this procedure is not likely to be employed at all for future Covid claims. However JR was brought by Claimants challenging the lawfulness of the government's decisions with respect to patients discharged from hospitals to care homes at the height of the Covid pandemic. The decision given by the Court may provide limited assistance to civil as opposed to an administrative claim. That case was *R (Gardner and Harris) v Secretary of State for Health and Social Care and Others* [2022] EWHC 967. It is covered in chapter 3. However it should be noted that the claim was met with limited success with respect to the common law claim over the removal of Covid infected patients from hospital into care homes. The human rights claim failed and the judicial review was unsuccessful. The court recognised that the Government was making decisions against a background of rapidly developing science under much pressure. The government's decision to transfer patients was lawful but the planning for those who were discharged was defective. The policy regarding care homes was irrational in failing to advise that an asymptomatic patient should isolate in a care home for 14 days.

It is noteworthy that the claim was financed via crowd-funding and at a preliminary hearing, Linden J granted a costs-capping order. He was moved by the impact the government's decision had on vulnerable people and their families whilst raising issues of law of real and general importance. Were it not for these two factors, one might imagine the case would not have been brought.

Nevertheless it is useful to know about the possibility of challenging decisions that may impact on someone's care. A Local authority has obligations under the *Care Act 2014* ('CA') to provide care, support and accommodation (section 18). In *R (SB and SBO) v London Borough of Newham*, 18.10.2023, the Local Authority terminated the provision of accommodation, contending that it had no obligation to meet housing needs under the CA, as the Claimants were entitled to support under s.95 *Immigration and Asylum Act 1999.* Such decision was unlawful and the decision withdrawing accommodation quashed.

CHAPTER SIX

PROCEDURE

6.1 PRE-ISSUE

Firstly an apology. This chapter contains lots of acronyms. Law is not immune and as the case management service moves inexorably to online platforms – hastened following the pandemic – digitisation increases their number.

Claimants almost universally require recognition that a wrong has been done to them, some assurance that improvements have been made to learn from mistakes and adequate recompense to reflect pain and suffering and reimbursement of financial losses. Commencing Court proceedings leading to a trial reflects failures by both/all parties. It takes time – anything from 2 to 4 years and is costly. Anything that can achieve settlement that takes the stresses and strains out of the system must be beneficial for all. This Chapter explores the procedures necessary to explore a claim and bring proceedings if necessary. This is an overview as the Civil Procedure Rules set out procedure and may be found at www.justice.gov.uk although the principal sections appear in appendix III.

Protocols

The Clinical Negligence Claims Agreement 2024 came into being on 27 August 2024 and is the successor to the COVID-19 Clinical Negligence Protocol 2020. Its aim is to improve claims management practices and thus save costs by avoiding litigation. The Agreement encapsulates all clinical negligence claims and also includes claims under the HRA 1998 and ECHR. The parties to the agreement, as before, are Claimants represented by Solicitors who are either members of AvMA's

Panel or Lawyers Service or members of SCIL. Defendants are those organisations indemnified by a defence organisation that is a signatory to the Agreement. This will largely be NHS Resolution but will include GPs indemnified by NHSR.

The key features included an extended Limitation period for certain cases by a further 12 months from 27 August 2024; early disclosure to help narrow the issues and reduce investigation costs; provide full disclosure both before and after issue of proceedings; greater use and acceptance of electronic communications, especially service of proceedings by email; and encouragement of pre-action discussions and dispute resolution to avoid unnecessary litigation.

The changes to the Limitation period are an important part of the Agreement and are especially pertinent to Covid-related claims. Claimants and their Solicitors who are not a party to the Agreement do not have the benefit of an automatic extension to the Limitation period and therefore will need to request and agree with the Defendant in writing an extension. In those cases, the expectation is that a reasonable limitation extension of up to 6 months will be agreed.

The Limitation date for any claims under the HRA 1998 or ECHR will be the same as under the *Law Reform (Miscellaneous Provisions)* Act 1934 and the *Fatal Accidents Act* 1976. This means that dependants of the deceased will have **three** years from the date of death to bring a claim. That is subject to the proviso that the deceased would have been within the limitation period when they could have brought a claim, i.e. within three years of injury or three years of date of knowledge.

Most importantly the agreement provides that before issue of proceedings, the parties should '*endeavour to actively engage in the consideration of mutual without prejudice exchange of liability evidence*'. That does seem beneficial on its face but there are more risks to Claimants, it is suggested. Some Defendants, at least in the initial stages, have obtained short form reports addressing liability. Essentially they are similar in content and detail to Claimants' screening reports that are usually obtained at the beginning of a case to ascertain viability. But they are not detailed reports and certainly not Court compliant (as per PD 35). The danger is that by the time without prejudice exchange of reports takes place, the Claimant has obtained full breach and causation reports which are disclosed in exchange for short form reports from the Defendant. It is not really 'cards on the table' transparency as it enables the Defendant to then instruct its experts to address the Claimants' arguments in its full Part 35 compliant breach/causation reports. And the Claimant gets little in return as the Defendants' short form reports do not develop the Defendants' arguments and may not even represent the experts that the Defendant relies upon. A savvy Claimant will require an assurance that its reports are not disclosed to the Defendants' experts (at least during the early exchange period). In reality though, the Defendants' legal team will simply instruct their experts to advise accordingly having had the benefit of learning the Claimants' arguments.

So how may this risk be circumnavigated? Claimants should ensure that The Defendants have obtained full breach/causation reports and will disclose them. Alternatively if their intention is to rely upon short form reports then the Claimant should disclose either an abridged version of its full reports or disclose their screening reports. That seems to miss the point as the thinking is to try and head off further litigation so leading to settlement. But brief reports are unlikely to add that much.

For Claimants who are not signatories to the Clinical Negligence Claims Agreement, it is anticipated that they and Defendants will wish to mirror some of its provisions as examples of good working practice. In particular early consideration should be given to settlement discussions, possibly even before the issue of proceedings. In previous times, it could be galling to attend ADR and find that proposals for settlement advanced by the Claimant were rebuffed on the basis that instructions needed to be sought from the Defendant's insurer/NHSLA/indemnifier. Any settlement meeting should be attended by (or at least be available remotely) a representative having authority to agree damages and with a sufficient reserve to do so.

Inevitably the expectations of Claimants are likely to comfortably exceed the limit of authority that Defendants are prepared to discuss. Should a meeting narrow the issues but not get over the line then the parties may reconvene on a future date.

The Pre-Action Protocol for the Resolution of Clinical Disputes ('the protocol') recommends a Stocktake before issue of proceedings to enable the parties to review their positions. Essentially to try and avoid Court action at all costs. While the Courts encourage Alternative Dispute Resolution (ADR) it is recognised that no party should be forced to mediate, though a failure to consider it may be deemed unreasonable by a Court and could lead to costs sanctions. If a stocktake is unsuccessful and no settlement is achieved, the parties will be required or perhaps encouraged to engage in Neutral Evaluation. Sanctions may apply for non-observance. So a rush to issuing proceedings could result in a reduction of fixed costs. If the Defendant it at fault, Claimant's damages may be increased.

The Civil Procedure (Amendment No. 3) Rules 2024 effective from 1 October 2024 confirm that the Overriding objective must now encourage the parties to use ADR, especially following the Court of Appeal decision in *James Churchill v Merthyr Tydfil County Borough Council*. The Civil Procedure Rules at 44.2(5) provides that the court can take into account a failure to comply with a order for ADR when reflecting on costs and conduct. Those Defendants that frustrate the objectives are on notice.

Meeting the Claimant

Who will that be? Either the injured party if they are able to attend a Solicitors' office and have capacity to give instructions. If the case concerns a fatality then usually the instructing client is the Personal Representative who intends – or has obtained – Letters of Administration where there is no will. An executor/executrix appointed by a will needs to prove it and that means obtaining a grant of probate.

Once a grant has been obtained or Letters of Appointment, then they have authority to act as the Claimant and to issue proceedings (pursuant to *Law Reform Miscellaneous Provisions Act 1934)*.

Funding/costs. Funding will need to be discussed. Most Claimants will wish to proceed via a Conditional Fee Agreement (CFA), colloquially known as 'no win no fee'. That and the terms of business agreement ('client care') must be agreed and signed. Anticipated costs must be raised and whether the client will need to pay any fees on account of disbursements. No one really knows how viable a clinical negligence claim becomes until screening expert reports on liability and causation are obtained. Even then, there may be great uncertainty. Although there has been consultation on fixed recoverable costs (FRC) for lower value clinical negligence claims below a settlement value of £25,000.00, the Civil Procedure Amendment Rules, thus far, have made no provision for changes, though they are expected imminently at the time of going to press. It is most likely to apply where there are open admissions of liability.

It is expected that exceptions to FRC will apply: in cases of 2 or more Defendants; where 3 or more expert reports on breach of duty and causation are required; where the Defendant raises limitation; claims arising from still birth and neonatal death; and cases where the Claimant undertakes the case themselves (Litigants in person). As ever with law, these details are subject to change.

Insurance. Currently solicitors often advise that where a CFA is taken out then the client may benefit from an after the event insurance policy (ATE). This generally provides that expenses (disbursements) are indemnified in the event that should a claim fail or have to be discontinued, then the ATE insurer will pay out for incurred disbursements on conclusion of the case. The insurers do not actually pay for the cost of disbursements upfront – it's a contingency only where the claim fails. They often will also indemnify against the Claimant having to pay any adverse costs to the Defendant. This is a version of loser pays the winner's costs. That could apply where there is:

- discontinuance against a Defendant when a claim fails, albeit adverse costs is unlikely

- where an interim (interlocutory) application has been made (unnecessarily) and the Defendant is awarded its costs;

- where the Claimant rejects a Part 36 offer of settlement and fails to recover more than that offer;

- where a claim (currently only personal injury) is inflated in value to take it out of the fixed costs regime;

- where the Claimant loses at trial in circumstances that the Court considers that there was misconduct that displaces the normal rule of one way qualified costs shifting (QOCS).[69]

Most ATE insurers currently will not provide inception cover at the outset until they have seen supportive screening reports and perhaps a provisional opinion from a barrister (Counsel) on merit. Perhaps they may require an indication on quantum, though this will be difficult in the early stages when little research has been undertaken. Claimants may be required to fund screening reports themselves. It may be that solicitors will be reluctant to enter into a CFA until they have obtained supportive evidence to proceed. Some may require a client to be privately funding at the outset until such preliminary evidence is obtained; others may take the risk and fund the cost of expert reports and other disbursements themselves. One can foresee issues on preliminary valuation of the claim. Claimants will be anxious to ensure

[69] CPR 44.15 provides QOCS protection (a 'shield') to Claimants who do not have to pay Defendant's costs where the Claimant loses the claim. In very rare circumstances the QOCS shield can be removed from the Claimant if they obstructed the just disposal of proceedings rendering a fair trial impossible. This could be where the Claimant was 'fundamentally dishonest'.

their case is outwith FRC whilst Defendants will argue the opposite. Once proceedings have been issued, the arguments may be finessed at a Case management and Costs Conference (CCMC).

With FRC on the horizon, ATE insurers will need to revise their model because it is expected that Counsel's fees may not be recoverable. If a Claimant is expected to put forward an offer of settlement with their Letter of Claim then most likely they will need to obtain detailed expert reports on breach of duty and causation, rather than screening reports. And the costs go up. If it transpires that the claim is not viable at this stage then there must be clarity as to who will be paying for those disbursements.

Dependant on how the first interview proceeds with the client, it may well be that they will wish to reflect on the initial discussions about process and funding. There is a lot to take in and they may wish to review the Solicitor's explanatory letter. They should be encouraged to read in their own time and reflect on the client care and CFA funding agreement. Indeed if they decide to sign outside the Solicitors' office, the client has a cooling off period of 14 days[70] unless they elect to forego this usual cancellation period.

<u>Medical records</u>. Medical records must be obtained shortly after the first consultation with the client. Careful review of care, GP and hospital records for continuity and consistency. Where terminology is not understood, it is helpful to have a basic medical dictionary or medical textbook. The Oxford handbook guides are helpful, and there is one on Respiratory Nursing. If a Solicitors' Practice is instructed they may employ in-house nurses or medico-legal assistants to note relevant entries, sort and paginate. Alternatively there are medical records and pagination agencies who employ staff familiar with clinical records who will undertake this task and prepare a synopsis. They may even have

70 The Consumer Contract (Information, Cancellation and additional Charges) Regulations 2013

access to a database of experts who will prepare a brief overview and highlight issues for consideration.

Whether the medical records are obtained first before taking a witness statement from the Claimant is personal choice; the author prefers to take a first draft as that tends to focus on the salient issues for reviewing the records. When it comes to care records, the emphasis will not necessarily be on the clinical notes but rather the procedures and risk assessments instituted to guard against the risk of Covid infection and transmission. It is how Covid was contracted that is the issue, from whom and why did it occur? Were their lax procedures in place? A thorough understanding of the systems at the Care home will be necessary. The clinical notes are important to learn about underlying health conditions. Any co-morbidities should be cross-referenced in particular with the GP records to gain a greater understanding of vulnerabilities.

If there has been an inquest, Solicitors or Counsel may have represented the family and will possess statements and medical reports. If there was no legal representation, the Coroner is usually happy to disclose a bundle of documents. This may provide a useful insight into the care of the deceased, even where no blame is attached – as that is not the Coroner's remit. Systemic issues may be revealed in procedures or even failings that impact on the deceased's care. It should not be assumed that simply where a Coroner gives a verdict of 'natural causes' that that implies there is no negligence claim to answer.

<u>Witness statement</u>. Following a review of the medical records, a further appointment with the client is indicated to discuss the findings and where necessary to update the witness statement. It may be that further witnesses have been identified. The prospect of obtaining a statement from someone employed at the Care home is slight. But they may have moved on and could be more willing to cooperate. CPR PD 32 sets out the rules governing witness statements. A statement must be factual addressing matters within the knowledge of the witness, not opinion or conjecture. If made on information and belief then the

statement should confirm this position. It should try to be concise, addressing matters in chronological order. Sub-headings are helpful to guide the reader. Content must be relevant and not meander. So for a care home resident, it should cover their background about admission into the care home; guidance that they have been given about Covid, any precautions and their understanding of procedures in place at the care home. It needs to address medical history and their symptomology, examinations by nurse and medical practitioners, diagnosis and treatment. Details about physical and psychological suffering should be included. How has contracting Covid affected their life? Do they suffer from long Covid? Have their care needs increased? Has their confidence been affected? What about the impact on visits? Have their been any financial losses sustained by them or others visiting them? Sometimes a chronology is helpful but only where the Claimant recalls specific dates. When proofing a witness, one must be mindful that the focus is on trying to prove liability and quantum, or at least seeking to assist expert witnesses. It could well be that two statements are taken from the Claimant, firstly addressing breach of duty and secondly on quantum. Claims brought on behalf of the estate of a deceased are clearly more difficult for the obvious fact that evidence will not be first hand. A statement containing hearsay is permissible but unlikely to be persuasive. Where a family member has been closely involved with the deceased's care and can speak as to their deterioration and how they managed before their illness, then this is clearly relevant. They may also wish to comment on any involvement in an inquest. Their statement will need to detail financial losses, especially where there are dependency claims. Ultimately for a statement to assist the Court or to enable the parties to conclude a settlement, it must be truthful, reliable, relevant and cogent.

With a signed statement and possession of a full paginated set of clinical and care records, you are ready to instruct an expert. Such is addressed in chapter 2.5.

Letter of Notification and Letter of Claim

Once the correct Defendant has been identified and their indemnity organisation (such as NHSLA representing an NHS Trust) or insurer, the Clinical Disputes Protocol suggests that the Claimant may wish to send a Letter of Notification to them. This fires the starting gun alerting the Defendant to a prospective claim; identifying that a claim in negligence, breach of duty or breach of human rights as appropriate will be forthcoming. The Defendant should acknowledge receipt within 14 days. They may then commence investigations by obtaining their own factual and expert evidence.

The Letter of Claim (LOC) follows and goes to the heart of the matter. This sets out the details of the Claimant, their injuries and losses and the legal framework alleging the cause of action. A template adopting the format from the Protocol appears at Appendix II.

The Letter of Response (LOR) should follow within 4 months unless the Defendant has requested an extension. It should set out the Defendant's position on breach of duty and causation. It may disclose some expert evidence in support but in all likelihood this will not occur until there has been mutual exchange with the Claimant and on a without prejudice basis.

ADR/Part 36. In the (unlikely) event of full admissions on liability then an offer letter of settlement may be forthcoming. If not, then the parties should consider whether they have sufficient expert evidence, witness statements, and schedules of loss to consider a settlement meeting. If the Defendants make partial admissions or even full denials, the Claimant may consider broaching ADR to see if settlement is achievable or at least for the issues to be narrowed. With changes made to the Civil Procedure Rules to promote the use of ADR, the courts will consider at the directions stage (post issue) whether to order or encourage the parties to participate in ADR[71]. This may be mediation or Early Neutral Evaluation. It may even constitute without prejudice discussions between the parties. The author prefers more formal discussions as they impart a level of seriousness and intent that may be lacking through exchange of emails or telephone discussions – they may simply act as a sounding board and no more. Anyway the parties can always make Part 36 offers of settlement. If the Claimant is ready to make an early Part 36 offer at the LOC stage then paragraph 3.26 of the protocol indicates that the Defendant should respond in its LOR. The Defendant may choose to make a Part 36 offer of its own volition. This may include any costs incurred to date. It may be expected that with forthcoming changes to lower value clinical negligence claims that Defendants may find such inclusive offers to be more attractive. It is notable from the protocol under paragraph 3.26 that any offer made by the Defendant should be a Part 36 offer as distinct from say a Calderbank 'without prejudice save as to costs' offer. If an offer is made, then sufficient medical or other evidence should be disclosed to allow the Claimant to properly consider the offer.

So the parties agree to explore ADR. Increasingly such meetings take place remotely. The parties should agree in advance the ambit of any discussions and provide advance disclosure, statements and expert reports together with a schedule of loss. There should be caution as to whether the parties are exchanging all of their evidence at this stage. If there is doubt, arrangements may be made for an in-person 'round table' meeting when reports may be handed over only for the day. This may be impracticable where the claim has more modest value. As a

---

71 CPR 1: covers the overriding objective of '*enabling the court to deal with cases justly and at proportionate cost… (f) promoting or using alternative dispute resolution*'.

CPR 1.4(2)(e) covers the court's case management powers, including '*ordering or encouraging the parties to use and facilitating the use of, alternative dispute resolution*'.

generality the Claimant prepares their schedule at their high-water mark, the Defendant at low water. It may be helpful to work through your own schedule and make deductions to reflect the counter schedule where their heads of loss are reasonable. The Claimant's Schedule still reflects a full liability assessment so it may be permissible to make further deductions to reflect any litigation risk in the event breach of duty and causation are in dispute. At this stage of play expert reports may be limited and there will not have been a meeting of experts to produce a joint report. Compromise may be the order of the day if settlement is achievable.

6.2 ISSUE/POST-ISSUE

If following a stock-take the parties remain entrenched and the Claimant has given 28 days' notice of their intention to issue proceedings, then the Claim Form and Particulars of Claim must be drafted.

Details of starting the claim are set out in CPR PD 51ZB.

For a Claimant represented by a law firm, a claim is issued using the Damages Claims Portal ('DCP') – an online portal. This requires an account with MyHMCTS and a court fee to be paid. For the purposes of limitation, the claim is brought at the point at which the claim is issued and the court fee is paid. There is no guarantee that the court will issue the claim immediately so Claimants must arrange for issue in good time before the limitation period is due to expire. Once uploaded, the Court provides the Claimant with the issued claim form via the DCP. The Claimant is responsible for notifying the Defendant, constituting service of proceedings under CPR 7.5(1). Service must be effected by the Claimant within 4 **months** of issue, otherwise his claim will be automatically struck out. If the Claimant needs more than 4 months to serve his statement of case then an application for an extension of time must be made on paper to the Civil National Business

Centre (CNBC) in Northampton. At this point the case drops out of the portal and proceeds in accordance with the old system set out in Part 7 of the CPR.

There are situations when the DCP does not have to be used, the most common of which are:

- *For Litigants in Person.
- *Claims where the Defendant is based in Wales.
- *Claims that qualify for the fee remission scheme.
- Claims by a protected party.
- Claims against three or more Defendants
- Claims where the Claimant has Legal Aid

In these situations, claims are issued using the old procedure via the CNBC under Part 7 of the CPR. 'Old' as preceding 4th April 2022. In fact the digitised process (at least currently but it is intended that all aspects of trial preparation will be rolled out digitally in due course) for most clinical negligence claims will fall out of the DCP following the issue of Directions and reunite with the CNBC, or transfer to the County Court hearing centre.

Following issue in the DCP, the Defendant replies; if they admit all or part of the claim then the claim automatically transfers out of the DCP to continue in the CNBC under Part 7 of the CPR. If both breach of duty and causation are admitted the claim is then allocated to the Intermediate Track[72] for directions for assessment of damages. If the

72 CPR 26.9(10) provides that clinical negligence claims are allocated to the multi track unless there has been a full admission of liability in the Letter of Response

Defendant intends to defend, they have 14 days if they do not upload an acknowledgement or 28 days if they do, to submit their Defence and Direction Questionnaire ('DQ'). The Claimant must indicate whether they want to continue with the claim, and assuming that is the case, provide hearing information within 28 days of the Defence in its own DQ. The Claimant then has 14 days or 28 days to file its DQ dependant on whether the claim is allocated to the Fast track, the Intermediate track or the Multi track. Presently it is anticipated that clinical negligence claims will be allocated to the Multi track. The parties should try and agree proposed directions contained within their DQ's.

If an application needs to be made (such as to extend time for service of the Claim Form, for example), then it must be made through the DCP. This is normally made on notice to the Defendant but if an application is made without notice, the application is first referred to a judge for consideration. The Defendant should respond within 5 days of notification.

Paper applications remain for cases pre-issue of proceedings in which case it is filed with the CNBC. If an order has already been made at a County Court hearing centre, then application should be made there.

If a case is allocated to the Fast track, (perhaps brought only as a personal injury claim) then a Trial readiness certificate must be completed. Once submitted, the court shall fix the date for trial and give any directions, including a trial timetable (paragraph 7.6 of PD 51ZB). Reforms are expected when fixed costs apply to clinical negligence claims for damages under £25,000.00 ('the Lower Damages Clinical Negligence Fixed Recoverable Cost, LDFRC'). For damages claimed at between £25,000.00 to £100,000.00, allocation is expected to be made to the Intermediate Track. Currently the Intermediate track only applies to clinical negligence cases where full admissions on breach of duty and causation are made in the Letter of Response[73]. Then fixed

73 ibid

costs apply to those claims where the incident/accident occurred after 1st October 2023. Naturally there is an exception and that would apply where 3 or more experts are required, in which case the claim remains in the Multi track. This is unlikely where only quantum remains to be determined. It may be anticipated that there will be lively argument as to what track a clinical negligence claim should be allocated. For this will determine the costs that ultimately may be recovered. For intermediate track cases, there are 4 complexity bands[74] dependant on the issues in dispute that will determine the level of fixed recoverable costs.[75]

Costs Management. Multi track cases, for which we are presently concerned, transfer out of the DCP to the CNBC. They then follow the procedure laid out in Part 7 of the CPR. A costs and case management conference hearing will be listed. This will address directions for trial, if not already determined, and a costs budget. The budget addresses phases in the litigation for the legal costs incurred by the Solicitor and the disbursements in the case. Sections are divided into:

a) Pre-action

b) Issues/statements of case

c) CMC

d) Disclosure

e) Witness statements

f) Expert reports

g) PTR

---

74 CPR 26.16

75 CPR 45.50 Table 14

h) Trial preparation

i) Trial

j) ADR/Settlement

A detailed costs budget should be drafted. Costs management is set out in PD 3D; Precedent H is annexed to the Practice Direction. Unless the conducting lawyer has experience (and the software) to undertake this task, it may be better left to a costs lawyer (draftsperson) to complete. The Court is concerned to ensure that costs are *reasonable and proportionate*[76]. In determining whether costs are proportionate, the Court may follow the guidance given in *West v Stockport NHS Foundation Trust*,[77] frequently known as the 'step back' approach:

1. Assess the claim for costs on a line-by-line basis, assessing their reasonableness;
2. The global figure is then assessed by reference to the factors in CPR 44.3(5) and CPR 44.4(1) to determine whether proportionate. If it is then the assessment is complete, otherwise;
3. A further assessment looking at specific categories of costs.

In essence the Court should consider the amount of costs, complexity, conduct, vulnerability and specialised knowledge. Invariably when reviewing the Claimant's and Defendant's respective costs budgets, there will be considerable disparity. That should not be considered unusual given the preliminary investigations undertaken by the Claimant, the level of disbursements such as Court fees, ATE insurance premiums and experts' reports. Defendants, reflecting their purchasing power, sometimes have arrangements with experts for reduced fees. The

[76] PD 3D, para 12

[77] [2019] EWCA Civ 1220

court should not perform a comparative exercise between the budgets even though Defendants frequently invite them to do so.

Many of the orders that the Court will make are viewed through the prism of cost effectiveness.

Case management. The Court when giving directions for the further conduct of the case up to and including trial will have regard to the parties' DQ's as they will contain draft directions and address the issue of experts, witnesses and arrangements for trial. Model Directions for a clinical negligence claim where breach of duty, causation and quantum are all in dispute appears at appendix III. It may be hoped that the parties can reach agreement on directions and costs budgets. Frequent areas of contention may reflect allocation to track, complexity band and the specialism and number of experts to be relied upon. This impacts costs and proportionality. In a contested clinical negligence claim, allocation should be Multi track[78]. Defendants may try and argue that a care home claim is really a personal injury claim and therefore should be a Fast track (or Intermediate track) case. The starting point is the definition in the Protocol for Clinical Disputes:

> '*1.1 This Protocol is intended to apply to all claims against hospitals, GPs, dentists and other healthcare providers (both NHS and private) which involve an injury that is alleged to be the result of clinical negligence…'*
>
> *1.2 This Protocol is intended to be sufficiently broad-based and flexible to apply to all sectors of healthcare, both public and private.'*

As we are talking about the impact that Covid has had on a resident/patient in a healthcare setting and the complexity of medical evidence that is likely with issues on breach of duty and causation, the Courts should be persuaded that the Multi track is appropriate.

78 CPR 26.9(10)

Guidance may be reached from the LOR and the Defence as to what allegations are rebutted.

In preparing for a hearing the court will expect to receive a case management bundle. This will include a case summary, draft directions, costs budget and skeleton argument.

The permission for appointment of experts often divides opinion and this can be pertinent to breach and causation reports. After all, the Defendant will not be that perturbed if a Claimant cannot prove his/her case for lack of evidence. CPR 35.4(1) provides that no party may call an expert or put in evidence an expert's report without the court's permission. The Court will consider CPR 35.1 – *'expert evidence shall be restricted to that which is reasonably required to resolve the proceedings'.* On a simple level that may mean only one expert on breach of duty and one on causation – perhaps a nurse practitioner for the former and a physician in elderly care for the latter. But that does not address the exceptional circumstances of the pandemic and the possibility that further experts may be required – as explored in Chapter 2.5. To guard against the risk that the court will restrict the Claimant's expert evidence, one may consider appending some liability expert reports with the Particulars of claim. Normally the Claimant would only disclose a condition and prognosis report at that stage.

The Court may explore with the parties whether a single joint expert is indicated. This would clearly save costs but one party may be not accept the opinion in which case do they abandon that expert and seek permission from the Court to instruct another? If it is likely to affect the trial date then almost certainly the Court will not depart from a single joint expert's opinion. The overriding objective and fairness will be the factors under consideration. Though an application to instruct a different expert was successful in *Daniels v Walker*[79] but failed in *Bulic v*

[79] [2000] EWCA Civ 508

Harwoods[80] where the Court examined the relevance and technical nature of the evidence. Often a party may lose confidence in the expert perhaps because they have not understood their instructions or appear to lack balance. Such could be revealed by asking supplemental questions.

Challenging case management decisions is difficult. Will it be a variation or appeal? Case management decisions are not 'rigid tramlines'[81] Is there any prejudice to a party? Have the expert reports been reviewed and given due consideration as to their significance? The judge enjoys a wide ambit of discretion. Should an appeal be pursued then the procedure is set out in PD 52A, paragraph 4.6. In deciding whether permission to appeal is granted, the court will have regard to:

- whether the issue is of sufficient significance to justify the costs of an appeal
- procedural consequences of an appeal
- whether it would be more convenient to determine the issue at trial.

Clearly grounds for appeal must be substantial and go to the heart of justice and fairness. A cost management decision was appealed in *Easteye Limited v Malhorta Property Investments Limited & Others.*[82] This was a property dispute but the principles apply equally to personal injury. The court did not allow a budget for the instruction of leading Counsel. On appeal, the judge observed that it was necessary to establish that the lower court made an decision that was so unreasoned as to be unfair, or took into account irrelevant material, or relevant matters were ignored or wrong on a question of principle. The court

80 [2012] EWHC 3657

81 Oyston & Anor v Rubin & Anor [2021] EWHC 448 (Ch)

82 [2019] EWHC 2820 (Ch)

did give an olive branch to the unsuccessful claimant in that there may be a 'good reason' to depart from the budget should leading counsel be instructed.

Following the issue of directions and assessing the parties' costs budget, the Court will most likely enquire about ADR.[83] Arguments by the Defendant that the claim is defended are unlikely to impress as a reason for rejection. The Court my consider the lack of interest in ADR as a ground to restrict costs under CPR 44 as conduct issues. They may invite the parties to stay proceedings until ADR has taken place.

6.3 SETTLEMENT/TRIAL

So you are at the doors of the court, all overtures to settle have been rebuffed.

The parties have completed their pre-trial checklists and the court has listed for a pre-trial review (PTR) hearing. Have all directions been complied with? By this stage the Court will have a bundle that includes the joint statements from the experts, the final schedules of loss and a case summary. The judge will discuss any particular arrangements for witnesses, whether any of the expert evidence is now agreed, so dispensing with their attendance. Dependant on the previous directions, permission to call oral expert evidence may need to be considered at the PTR. They will enquire about quantum and whether this is capable of being agreed, or at least general damages for pain, suffering and loss of amenity. Essentially they want to know what issues may be narrowed and agreed, and what is left for them to try. The judge may still encourage the parties to promote settlement.

---

[83] CPR 29: *(1A) When giving directions the court must consider whether to order or encourage the parties to participate in alternative dispute resolution.*

Given where we are, that may appear increasingly remote. If only quantum is in issue, that can be compromised. Where the Defendant maintains a firm denial on breach and/or causation how can settlement be effected? Both parties will possess supportive expert reports and the joint statements from the experts presumably maintain their initial positions without concessions. We have a 'stand-off'. The Defendant's representative may resort to rhetoric – the Claimant cannot succeed; the Defendant's expert evidence is stronger, more persuasive, better qualified, more experienced... That will not persuade a Claimant to discontinue. A Defendant making threats to seek costs if the Claimant loses at trial should not happen in a properly advanced case. But it may form part of their negotiating style. The QOCS's shield is very rarely displaced and will not occur simply because the Court prefers one expert to another. Of course intransigence is not necessarily the preserve of Defendants. A Claimant holding out for what could be perceived as an excessive and over-optimistic valuation of their claim is not unknown. That however is addressed by a well-pitched Part 36 offer from the Defendant. And then the Claimant may be at risk of paying adverse costs should they reject the offer.

Claimants should have made offers of settlement at the earliest opportunity when the claim was capable of being valued. Until trial, offers may continue to be made, though they may have less impact when a Defendant has incurred a substantial amount of costs with less incentive to settle.

Litigation risk exists for both parties, though commercial risk is far greater for Claimants. Only 0.4% of clinical negligence cases reach trial. But the balance at trial is very much in favour of Defendants. According to NHS Resolution's report for 2023/2024, 50 cases went to trial of which 17 Claimants were successful. The odds of losing are stacked two to one based on that statistic. Yet for settlements achieved before the issue of proceedings NHSR settled 51% of claims.

It must be appreciated that this applies to clinical negligence claims largely against Hospital NHS Trusts; it may incorporate claims against

GP's and Dentists during the pandemic period and its aftermath. Claims against care homes that are largely owned in the private sector will not form part of that matrix.

With fixed costs, it may be expected that more cases will settle pre-issue as there is a clear economic incentive for Defendants to do so, even making 'commercial offers'. Trials will become a rare phenomenon and with that, one can see the prospects of success for Claimants diminishing further.

Claimants may need to make more significant concessions than perhaps they want to do. This is where Calderbank without prejudice offers save as to costs may have merit. Costs may become a significant impediment close to trial. A Calderbank offer is a means of making an offer of damages and costs fully inclusive. Certainly, careful discussions with the Claimant must proceed before making such an offer. The Claimant's lawyer and client must agree the elements comprising damages and that for costs. Clearly that does not need to be revealed to the Defendant but may represent the 'last throw of the dice' before trial. It is a means by which the Defendant's exposure to damages and costs is capped, perhaps significantly so, than were it to go to trial and lose. Such an offer may open a dialogue that hitherto was closed.

Counsel or Advocates for the parties are likely to become more closely involved as the trial approaches. There may have been conferences with the experts following receipt of the joint statements to finesse final arguments. Counsel will generally draft the skeleton argument and require the trial bundle in good time. If there have been no discussions with their counterpart, then they should be encouraged to have a without prejudice discussion about the evidence and the case generally. Much depends on their style; they may simply wish to get to the point and broke an offer. Sometimes a fresh approach can be revealing and break the impasse.

Round table meetings are less prevalent than they were before remote conferences. But there is value in meeting face to face. It will depend on geography and the health of the Claimant and/or family members. If they cannot attend then there is little to be gained by lawyers meeting in person. If it is possible, and representatives from the insurers or NHSLA attend, then perhaps progress is achievable.

Sometimes a settlement simply won't happen.

Trial bundles must be finalised and accord with PD 39A, paragraph 3.2:

- Skeleton arguments
- Case Summary and chronology
- Claim Form and statements of case
- Court Orders
- Witness statements
- Hearsay notices
- Expert reports, including joint statements
- Medical records (in separate bundles)

Most court bundles will be expected to be electronic bundles – some hearings may be remote, though much depends on the trial judge's preferences. The witness box will still have a paper bundle as some witnesses will have difficulty navigating an e-bundle. There should be agreement between the parties about content. Sometimes one party may require application notices to be incorporated, though provided the court order is included they alone should suffice. Documents must be admissible. If, for example, an expert refers to a report for which permission has not been given, should it be included? If it has not been disclosed in accordance with Part 31 then the prospect of the court attaching any weight to it are minimal. If the case management judge has denied permission for a particular expert then it becomes even more difficult to justify its inclusion. If included within the bundle then it will not be an agreed bundle. A party objecting to admissibility of a document should serve a written notice pursuant to CPR 32 PD 27.2. The risk is that the party wishing to rely on a document that is ruled inadmissible may incur an adverse costs order concerning any application notice and preliminary hearing. Where an expert provides footnotes or links to references then they should be obtained and annexed to the report.

On the morning of trial, assuming all experts attend and the parties are present, there is often some time before the case is heard to go though court etiquette, procedure and review any troubling issues. There may be an opportunity for Counsel to meet, and if not already determined, discuss whether anything further may be agreed. A last minute conference with experts to check their evidence may be beneficial.

The parties are called in and the trial commences. Details of advocacy are outwith this book's remit, though (plug alert), the reader is invited to explore this further, perhaps including the author's companion edition.

Ending this chapter on a positive note, let us assume that settlement has been achieved and the parties need to record terms of the agreement in a Consent Order, or should it be a Tomlin Order? The distinction lies in court approval and enforceability. A Consent order is an order of the court where judgment is entered, whilst a Tomlin order represents a contractual agreement between the parties. In the former, breach of its terms may constitute contempt of court whilst breach of a Tomlin order has the remedy of breach of contract. There are disadvantages of Consent Orders with respect to costs. The court does not have power to order that either party pays the other some or all of its costs where the case settles before trial. It is suitable for dismissal, discontinuance or withdrawal of proceedings. Once concluded and perfected, the court will not interfere with the terms. A Tomlin Order is in two parts; the first part is the court order which stays the proceedings and orders payment of costs. The second part – the Schedule records the agreement, including any confidentiality provisions and payment of damages, where appropriate. It will also normally address full settlement against all or any future actions arising from the same facts. As a binding contract, the provisions may be enforced between the parties without the need for fresh proceedings. It is particularly suitable where a claim is made against multiple Defendants where discontinuance applies against one or more as they may not recover adverse costs from damages. A Tomlin order is not an order to which CPR 44.14(1) applies.

The basic form of wording appears overleaf.

IN THE COUNTY COURT AT XXXX *Claim No.*

BETWEEN

MRS INJURED PARTY

Claimant

-and-

DEFENDANT CARE HOME LTD

Defendant

CONSENT ORDER

UPON the Parties to the Action consenting to the terms set out below

BY CONSENT IT IS ORDERED THAT

1. All further proceedings in this case be stayed upon the terms set out in the Schedule to this Order except for the purpose of enforcing the terms of this Agreement.

2. Either Party may apply to the court to enforce the terms of this Agreement without the need to commence new proceedings.

3. The Defendant do pay the Claimant's reasonable costs of this action to be assessed on the standard basis if not agreed.

SCHEDULE

a) The Defendant shall pay to the Claimant by way of damages, inclusive of interest, the sum of £X by [date] without admissions of liability and subject to confidentiality.

b) The said payment of £X is in full settlement of all or any actions she may have against the Defendant.

c) Upon payment of the said sum of £X this action do stand dismissed.

We hereby consent to the terms of this agreement.

Signed ....

Claimant/Solicitors Defendant/Solicitors

Date:

APPENDIX I

CIVIL PROCEDURE RULES 1998

An excerpt as there are 89 Parts to the CPR.

PART 1	Overriding Objective
PART 2	Application and Interpretation of the Rules
PART 3	The Court's Case and Costs Management Powers
PART 4	Forms
PART 5	Court Documents
PART 6	Service of Documents
PART 7	How to Start Proceedings – the Claim Form
PART 8	Alternative Procedure for Claims
PART 9	Responding to Particulars of Claim – General
PART 10	Acknowledgment of Service
PART 11	Disputing the Court's Jurisdiction
PART 12	Default Judgment
PART 13	Settings Aside or Varying Default Judgment
PART 14	Admissions
PART 15	Defence and Reply

PART 16	Statements of Case
PART 17	Amendments to Statements of Case
PART 18	Further Information
PART 19	Parties and Group Litigation
PART 20	Counterclaims and other Additional Claims
PART 21	Children and Protected Parties
PART 22	Statements of Truth
PART 23	General Rules about Applications for Court Orders
PART 24	Summary Judgment
PART 25	Interim Remedies and Security for Costs
PART 26	Case Management – Preliminary Stage
PART 27	The Small Claims Track
PART 28	The Fast Track
PART 29	The Multi-Track
PART 30	Transfer
PART 31	Disclosure and Inspection of Documents
PART 32	Evidence
PART 33	Miscellaneous Rules about Evidence
PART 34	Witnesses, Depositions and Evidence for Foreign Courts
PART 35	Experts and Assessors

APPENDIX II

DRAFT LETTER OF CLAIM (FROM PROTOCOL)

To

Defendant

Dear Sirs

Letter of Claim Under the Clinical Disputes Protocol

[Claimant's Name] –v- [Defendant's Name]

We have been instructed on behalf of [Claimant's name] in relation to care received at the [name of Care home/Hospital NHS Foundation Trust/Local Authority] on [date]. Please let us know if you do not believe that you are the appropriate defendant or if you are aware of any other potential defendants.

Claimant's details

Full name, DoB, address, NHS Number

[Personal Representative's details]

Dates of allegedly negligent treatment

- Include chronology based on medical records.

Events giving rise to the claim:

- An outline of what happened, including details of other relevant treatments to the client by other healthcare providers.

Allegation of negligence [breach of statutory duty/ breach of human rights] and causal link with injuries:

- An outline of the allegations or a more detailed list in a complex case;
- An outline of the causal link between allegations and the injuries complained of;
- A copy of any supportive expert evidence (optional).

The Client's injuries, condition and future prognosis

- A copy of any supportive expert report (optional);
- Suggestions for rehabilitation;
- The discipline of any expert evidence obtained or proposed.

Clinical records (if not previously provided)

We enclose an index of all the relevant records that we hold. We shall be happy to provide copies of these on payment of our photocopying charges.

We enclose a request for copies of the following records which we believe that you hold. We confirm that we shall be responsible for your reasonable copying charges. Failure to provide these records may result in costs sanctions if proceedings are issued.

The likely value of the claim

- An outline of the main heads of damage, or, in straightforward cases, the details of loss;
- Part 36 settlement offer (optional);

- Suggestions for ADR.

Funding

[State method of funding and whether arrangement was entered into before or after April 2013.]

We enclose a further copy of this letter for you to pass to your insurer. We look forward to receiving an acknowledgment of this letter within 14 days and your Letter of Response within 4 months of the date on which this letter was received. We calculate the date for receipt of your Letter of Response to be [date].

Recoverable Benefits

The claimant's National Insurance Number will be sent to you in a separate envelope.

We look forward to hearing from you.

Yours faithfully

APPENDIX III

MODEL DIRECTIONS ORDER

On [date]

Before District Judge XXXX sitting in the County Court at XXXX

Upon hearing the solicitor for the Claimant and the solicitor for the Defendant and made the following Order

1) The claim is allocated to the Multi-Track and is assigned to District Judge XXXX for case management.

2) At all stages the parties must consider settling this litigation by any means of Alternative Dispute Resolution (including round table conferences, early neutral evaluation, mediation and arbitration); any party not engaging in any such means proposed by another is to serve a witness statement giving reasons within 21 days of receipt of that proposal. That witness statement must not be shown to the trial judge until questions of costs arise.

3) Documents are to be retained as follows:

   a) the parties must retain all electronically stored documents relating to the issues in this claim.

   b) The Defendant must retain the original clinical notes relating to the issues in this claim. The Defendant must give facilities for inspection by the Claimant, the Claimant's legal advisers and experts of these original notes on 7 days written notice.

c) Legible copies of the medical and educational records of the Claimant/Deceased are to be placed in a separate paginated bundle by the Claimant's solicitors and kept up to date. All references to medical notes are to be made by reference to the pages in that bundle.

4) Disclosure of documents relevant to the issues of breach of duty and causation and quantification of damages will be dealt with as follows:

   a) By 4pm on [date] both parties must give to each other standard disclosure of documents by list and category.

   b) By 4pm on [date] any request must be made to inspect the original of, or to provide a copy of, a disclosable document.

   c) Any such request unless objected to must be complied with within 14 days of the request.

   d) By 4pm on [date] each party must serve and file with the court a list of issues relevant to the search for and disclosure of electronically stored documents, or must confirm there are no such issues, following Practice Direction 31B.

5) Evidence of fact will be dealt with as follows:

   a) By 4pm on [date] both parties must serve on each other copies of the signed statements of themselves and of all witnesses on whom they intend to rely in respect of breach of duty and causation and all notices relating to evidence, including Civil Evidence Act notices.

   b) For the avoidance of doubt statements of all concerned with the relevant treatment and care of the Claimant must be included.

c) By 4pm on [date] both parties must serve on each other copies of the signed statements of themselves and of all witnesses on whom they intend to rely in respect of condition, prognosis and loss and all notices relating to evidence, including Civil Evidence Act notices.

d) Oral evidence will not be permitted at trial from a witness whose statement has not been served in accordance with this order or has been served late, except with permission from the Court.

e) Evidence of fact is limited to xx witnesses on behalf of each party.

f) Witness statements must not exceed xx pages of A4 length.

6) Expert evidence is directed as follows.

7) The parties have permission in respect of breach of duty and causation and quantification of damages to rely on the jointly instructed written evidence of an expert xxxx

a) By [date] the expert should be agreed and instructed, and if no expert has been Instructed by that date the Claimant must apply to court by 4pm the following day for further directions.

b) By [date] the expert will report to the instructing parties.

c) By [date] the parties may put written questions to the expert.

d) By [date] the expert will reply to the questions.

e) A copy of this order must be served on the expert by the Claimant with the expert's instructions.

f) A party seeking to call the expert to give oral evidence at trial must apply for permission to do so before pre-trial check lists are filed.

g) Unless the parties agree in writing or the Court orders otherwise, the fees and expenses of the expert shall be paid by the parties giving instructions for the report equally.

8) In respect of breach of duty and causation the parties each have permission to rely on the following written expert evidence:

a) The Claimant:

i) an expert in xxxx, namely Mr A, whose report must be served by [date].

ii) an expert in xxxx, namely Dr B, whose report must be served by [date].

iii) an expert in xxxx, namely Ms C, whose report must be served by [date]

b) The Defendant:

i) an expert xxxx, namely Mr AA, whose report must be served by [date].

ii) an expert xxxx, namely Mr BB, whose report must be served by [date].

iii) an expert xxxx, namely Ms C, whose report must be served by [date].

9) In respect of condition, prognosis and quantification of damages the parties (the Defendants acting jointly) each have permission to rely on the following written expert evidence:

a) The Claimant:

i) an expert in xxxx, namely Mr A, whose report must be served by [date].

ii) an expert in xxxx, namely Dr B, whose report must be served by [date].

iii) an expert in xxxx, namely Ms C, whose report must be served by [date].

b) The Defendant:

i) an expert in xxxx, namely Mr AA, whose report must be served by [date].

ii) an expert in xxxx, namely Mr BB, whose report must be served by [date].

iii) an expert in xxxx, namely Ms CC, whose report must be served by [date].

10) Unless the reports are agreed, there must be a without prejudice discussion between

the experts of like discipline by 4pm on [date] in which the experts will identify the issues between them and reach agreement if possible. The experts will prepare for the court and sign a statement of the issues on which they agree and on which they disagree with a summary of their reasons in accordance with Rule 35.12 Civil Procedure Rules, and each statement must be sent to the parties to be received by 4pm on [date] and in any event no later than 7 days after the discussion.

11) Unless otherwise agreed by all parties" solicitors, after consulting with the experts, a draft agenda which directs the experts to the

remaining issues relevant to the experts' discipline, as identified in the statements of case shall be prepared jointly by the Claimant's solicitors and experts and sent to the Defendant's solicitors for comment at least 35 days before the agreed date for the experts' discussions.

12) The Defendants shall within 21 days of receipt agree the Agenda, or propose amendments.

13) A copy of this order must be served on each expert with the expert's instructions.

14) The parties have permission to call oral evidence of the experts in xxxx limited to issues remaining in dispute between experts of like discipline.

15) Any unpublished literature upon which any expert witness proposes to rely must be served at the same time as service of his report together with a list of published literature. Any supplementary literature upon which any expert witness relies must be notified to all parties at least one month before trial. No expert witness may rely upon any publications that have not been disclosed in accordance with this order without the permission of the trial judge subject to costs as appropriate.

16) Experts will, at the time of producing their reports, incorporate details of any employment activity which raises a possible conflict of interest.

17) For the avoidance of doubt, experts do not require the authorisation of solicitor or counsel before signing a joint statement.

18) If an expert radically alters an opinion previously recorded, the joint statement should include a note or addendum by that expert explaining the change of opinion.

19) Schedules of Loss must be updated as follows:

   a) By 4pm on [date] the Claimant must send an up-to-date schedule of loss to the Defendant.

   b) By 4pm on [date] the Defendant, in the event of challenge, must send an up to date counter-schedule of loss to the Claimant.

   c) The schedule and counter-schedule must contain a statement setting out that party's case on the issue of periodical payments pursuant to Rule 41.5 Civil Procedure Rules.

20) The trial will be listed as follows.

   a) The trial window is between [date] and [date] inclusive.

   b) The estimated length of trial is xx days.

   c) By 4pm on [date] the parties must file with the court their availability for trial, preferably agreed with a nominated single point of contact. They will be notified of the time and place of trial.

   d) By 4pm on [date] pre-trial check lists must be sent to the court.

21) Pre-trial directions are as follows.

   a) There will be a pre-trial review 4 weeks before the trial window starts with a time estimate of 30 minutes.

b) The pre-trial review will be conducted by telephone, unless the court orders otherwise. The Claimant must make the relevant arrangements in accordance with Practice Direction 23A Civil Procedure Rules.

c) At least 3 clear days before the case management conference the Claimant must file and send to the Defendant preferably agreed and by email:

(i) any draft directions;

(ii) a case summary.

22) Not more than 7 nor less than 3 clear days before the trial, the Claimant must file at court and serve an indexed and paginated bundle of documents which complies with the requirements of Rule 39.5 Civil Procedure Rules and Practice Direction 39A. The parties must endeavour to agree the contents of the bundle before it is filed. The bundle will include a case summary and a chronology.

23) The parties must file with the court and exchange skeleton arguments at least three days before the trial, by email.

24) Costs in the case.

MORE BOOKS BY
LAW BRIEF PUBLISHING

A selection of our other titles available now:-

'A Practical Guide to Probation Breaches and Other Applications' by Mark Thomas
'A Practical Guide to Remarriage and Divorce' by Cordelia Williams & Claire Howard
'A Practical Guide to Privacy, Transparency, Reporting Restrictions and Closed Proceedings in the Court of Protection' by Laura Mannering
'Beaumont on Barristers – A Guide to Defending Disciplinary Proceedings (Second Edition)' by Marc Beaumont
'A Practical Guide to Payments for Environmental Services' by Ben Sharples
'A Practical Guide to the Law of Pregnancy and Maternity at Work' by Rebecca Thomas
'A Practical Guide to Redundancy – Second Edition' by Philip Hyland & Collette Moore
'A Practical Guide to International Issues for Scottish Family Lawyers' by Susie Mountain, Donna McKay, Ken MacDonald
'A Practical Guide to the Law on Deprivation of Liberty' by Ben Troke
'A Practical Guide to Rights over Airspace and Subsoil – Second Edition' by Daniel Gatty
'A Practical Guide to the Law in Relation to Inquests' by Ramya Nagesh
'A Practical Guide to the Construction and Rectification of Wills and Trust Instruments (Second Edition)' by Edward Hewitt
'A Practical Guide to Data Protection in Social Housing' by Clare Paterson
'A Practical Guide to Spousal Maintenance – Second Edition' by Liz Cowell
'A Practical Guide to International Parental Child Abduction Law (England and Wales)' by Dr Onyója Momoh
'A Practical Guide to Deprivation of British Citizenship' by Sean Ell
'A Practical Guide to Commercial Property Service Charges' by Rachel Garton
'A Practical Guide to Clinical Negligence – Third Edition' by Geoffrey Simpson-Scott (Geoff)
'A Practical Guide to the Rights of Grandparents in Children Proceedings – Second Edition' by Stuart Barlow

'The Electronic Communications Code: A Practical Guide – Second Edition' by Kerry Bretherton KC, James Castle, Mark Loveday
'A Practical Guide to the Independent School Standards – September 2023 Edition' by Sarah McKimm
'A Practical Guide to Estate Administration and Crypto Assets' by Richard Marshall
'A Practical Guide to Parental Alienation in Private and Public Law Children Cases' by Sam King QC & Frankie Shama
'Contested Heritage – Removing Art from Land and Historic Buildings' by Richard Harwood QC, Catherine Dobson, David Sawtell
'The Limits of Separate Legal Personality: When Those Running a Company Can Be Held Personally Liable for Losses Caused to Third Parties Outside of the Company' by Dr Mike Wilkinson
'A Practical Guide to Transgender Law' by Robin Moira White & Nicola Newbegin
'A Practical Guide to 'Stranded Spouses' in Family Law' by Mani Singh Basi
'A Practical Guide to Residential Freehold Conveyancing' by Lorraine Richardson
'A Practical Guide to Pensions on Divorce for Lawyers' by Bryan Scant
'A Practical Guide to Challenging Sham Marriage Allegations in Immigration Law' by Priya Solanki
'A Practical Guide to Digital Communications Evidence in Criminal Law' by Sam Willis
'A Practical Guide to Legal Rights in Scotland' by Sarah-Jane Macdonald
'A Practical Guide to New Build Conveyancing' by Paul Sams & Rebecca East
'A Practical Guide to Inherited Wealth on Divorce' by Hayley Trim
'A Practical Guide to Practice Direction 12J and Domestic Abuse in Private Law Children Proceedings' by Rebecca Cross & Malvika Jaganmohan
'A Practical Guide to Confiscation and Restraint' by Narita Bahra QC, John Carl Townsend, David Winch
'A Practical Guide to the Law of Forests in Scotland' by Philip Buchan
'A Practical Guide to Health and Medical Cases in Immigration Law' by Rebecca Chapman & Miranda Butler
'A Practical Guide to Bad Character Evidence for Criminal Practitioners by Aparna Rao
'A Practical Guide to Extradition Law post-Brexit' by Myles Grandison et al
'A Practical Guide to Hoarding and Mental Health for Housing Lawyers' by Rachel Coyle

'Stephens on Contractual Indemnities' by Richard Stephens
'A Practical Guide to the EU Succession Regulation' by Richard Frimston
'A Practical Guide to Solicitor and Client Costs – Second Edition' by Robin Dunne
'Constructive Dismissal – Practice Pointers and Principles' by Benjimin Burgher
'A Practical Guide to Religion and Belief Discrimination Claims in the Workplace' by Kashif Ali
'A Practical Guide to the Law of Medical Treatment Decisions' by Ben Troke
'Fundamental Dishonesty and QOCS in Personal Injury Proceedings: Law and Practice' by Jake Rowley
'A Practical Guide to the Law in Relation to School Exclusions' by Charlotte Hadfield & Alice de Coverley
'A Practical Guide to Divorce for the Silver Separators' by Karin Walker
'The Right to be Forgotten – The Law and Practical Issues' by Melissa Stock
'A Practical Guide to Planning Law and Rights of Way in National Parks, the Broads and AONBs' by James Maurici QC, James Neill et al
'A Practical Guide to Election Law' by Tom Tabori
'A Practical Guide to the Law in Relation to Surrogacy' by Andrew Powell
'A Practical Guide to Claims Arising from Fatal Accidents – Second Edition' by James Patience
'A Practical Guide to Asbestos Claims' by Jonathan Owen & Gareth McAloon
'A Practical Guide to Stamp Duty Land Tax in England and Northern Ireland' by Suzanne O'Hara
'A Practical Guide to the Law of Farming Partnerships' by Philip Whitcomb
'A Practical Guide to the Law of Unlawful Eviction and Harassment – Second Edition' by Stephanie Lovegrove
'A Practical Guide to Costs in Personal Injury Claims – Second Edition' by Matthew Hoe
'A Practical Guide to the General Data Protection Regulation (GDPR) – Second Edition' by Keith Markham
'A Practical Guide to Working with Litigants in Person and McKenzie Friends in Family Cases' by Stuart Barlow
'Protecting Unregistered Brands: A Practical Guide to the Law of Passing Off' by Lorna Brazell
'A Practical Guide to Secondary Liability and Joint Enterprise Post-Jogee' by Joanne Cecil & James Mehigan

'A Practical Guide to the Pre-Action RTA Claims Protocol for Personal Injury Lawyers' by Antonia Ford
'A Practical Guide to Neighbour Disputes and the Law' by Alexander Walsh
'A Practical Guide to Coercive Control for Legal Practitioners and Victims' by Rachel Horman
'A Practical Guide to the Law of Driverless Cars – Second Edition'
by Alex Glassbrook, Emma Northey & Scarlett Milligan
'A Practical Guide to TOLATA Claims' by Greg Williams
'A Practical Guide to Elderly Law – Second Edition' by Justin Patten
'A Practical Guide to Responding to Housing Disrepair and Unfitness Claims' by Iain Wightwick
'A Practical Guide to the Law of Bullying and Harassment in the Workplace' by Philip Hyland
'How to Be a Freelance Solicitor: A Practical Guide to the SRA-Regulated Freelance Solicitor Model' by Paul Bennett
'A Practical Guide to Prison Injury Claims' by Malcolm Johnson
'A Practical Guide to Advising Clients at the Police Station' by Colin Stephen McKeown-Beaumont
'A Practical Guide to Antisocial Behaviour Injunctions – Second Edition' by Iain Wightwick
'Practical Mediation: A Guide for Mediators, Advocates, Advisers, Lawyers, and Students in Civil, Commercial, Business, Property, Workplace, and Employment Cases' by Jonathan Dingle with John Sephton
'The Mini-Pupillage Workbook' by David Boyle
'A Practical Guide to Crofting Law' by Brian Inkster
'A Practical Guide to the Law of Domain Names and Cybersquatting' by Andrew Clemson
'A Practical Guide to the Law of Gender Pay Gap Reporting' by Harini Iyengar
'NHS Whistleblowing and the Law' by Joseph England
'Employment Law and the Gig Economy' by Nigel Mackay & Annie Powell
'A Practical Guide to Noise Induced Hearing Loss (NIHL) Claims' by Andrew Mckie, Ian Skeate, Gareth McAloon
'An Introduction to Beauty Negligence Claims – A Practical Guide for the Personal Injury Practitioner' by Greg Almond
'Intercompany Agreements for Transfer Pricing Compliance' by Paul Sutton
'Zen and the Art of Mediation' by Martin Plowman
'A Practical Guide to Adoption for Family Lawyers' by Graham Pegg

www.ingramcontent.com/pod-product-compliance
Ingram Content Group UK Ltd.
Pitfield, Milton Keynes, MK11 3LW, UK
UKHW020142290926
15471UKWH00004B/655